# winning racquetball

## Arthur Shay
### with Chuck Leve

Contemporary Books, Inc.
Chicago

Published by Contemporary Books, Inc.
180 North Michigan Avenue, Chicago, Illinois 60601
Manufactured in the United States of America
Library of Congress Catalog Card Number: 77-80510
International Standard Book Number: 0-8092-8086-8 (cloth)
                                     0-8092-8062-0 (paper)

Published simultaneously in Canada by
Beaverbooks
953 Dillingham Road
Pickering, Ontario L1W 1Z7
Canada

# dedication

Long before Bob Kendler wrote the preface for this book, Chuck Leve and I both decided that Bob Kendler was the only person to whom we could dedicate *Winning Racquetball*. Bob's unselfish dedication—of himself, his time, his family's time, and his money—to the court sports has helped him make them an extension of his foresight, love, and enthusiasm. The fantastic growth of racquetball in this Bicentennial year is, in a sense, a present from Bob Kendler to his beloved country and its young people.

Arthur Shay

# contents

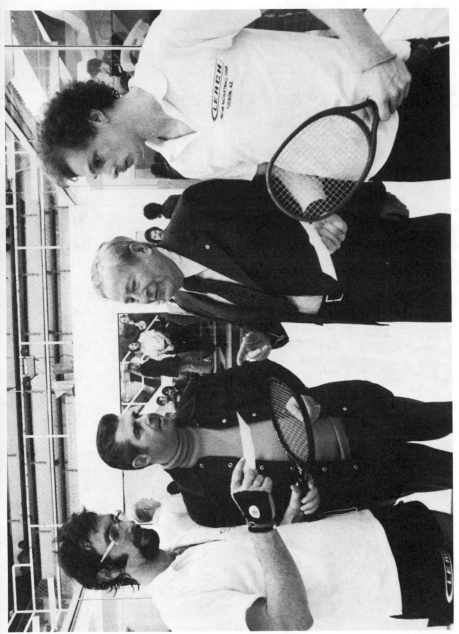

Pointing to the winner's check he has presented to Charlie Brumfield, USRA President Bob Kendler holds forth on the future of racquetball as Seamco President Al Mackie and runner-up Dave Bledsoe listen.

# preface

It was Disraeli who said, "A preface, being the entrance of a book, should invite by its beauty." Alas, I am not known in the world of four-wall sports as a writer of beautiful words. But let me substitute enthusiasm—and invite you to a feast—if you hunger for becoming a *winning* racquetball player.

When Arthur Shay asked me about the wisdom of doing a book on "winning racquetball" from his entrenchment as a part-time racquet-baller and a full-time photojournalist, I enthusiastically encouraged him. I knew and know Art to be a master of the sequence camera and the author-photographer of 32 books for children. His stock in trade is clarity and explanation, and thousands of his pictures—including 500 magazine covers—have appeared on *Sports Illustrated*, *Life*, *Time*, and elsewhere over the years. Difficult assignments never faze him.

He hold's *Life*'s record for Mafia stories—*fifty* of them! When I think of beautifully illustrated sports, I think of the canvases of LeRoy Nieman and the camera work of Arthur Shay. They both invariably capture the prowess of athletes, the driving strength in their bodies, the will that is whipped to success by competitive challenge.

Competition! One of our country's basic foundations. To me, the joy of participating in handball or racquetball has always been spiced by my—shall I say—strong (my opponents have sometimes said "paranoid") desire to *win*. As a three-times-a-week handballer or racquetballer—at age 71—my reputation as a go-for-broke winner has hardened. It just gets more difficult to win—and especially, to make the body go where the eyes, mind, and heart direct it. You've seen it on the screen or in the stadium—that determined bulling ahead for the extra yard by a Gale Sayers; the extra-effort slide toward the bag by a Pete Rose; Paul Haber or Fred Lewis turning an impossible retrieve into an aggressive corner kill on the handball court; Steve Serot flying through the air retrieving a Marty Hogan "pass." See the pictures of 17-year-old Marty Hogan beating 26-year-old reigning champ Charlie Brumfield for an illustration of sheer desire moving a young man to great heights. (Note: In line with the youth movement, these fine shots were made by Art Shay's 22-year-old assistant—his son Dick Shay!)

These are interesting times for sports. Sporting events themselves have clambered out of the arena through our papers, magazines, and screens into the very heart of the American family. I have seen my own beloved handball and racquetball climb into stratospheric levels of acceptance and participation. Other members of my family and good friends assure me that 25 million of us wield tennis rackets! Perhaps ironically, it is from this vast body of racqueteers that racquetball has been drawing some of its most ardent recruits. Many of them never saw a racquetball court until their tennis club installed a few down the far end. And they want to *win*!

"If you plan to write about winning," I advised Shay, "go to the winners. Interview Brumfield, Schmidtke, Serot, Hogan, Keeley, Rubenstein, Charlie Drake . . . But stay away from the psychophysiologists—the Zen theorists, the yoga types, the mystics." I'm not saying that the psychology of winning is above or beyond explanation or theory. What I'm saying is that mental gymnastics work for only a small proportion of winners. The vast majority of them work, work, work at their sport. To put this into perspective, Charlie Brumfield sometimes spends a five-hour day practicing *one single shot a thousand times!*

It is rewarding to me, glancing at *Winning Racquetball* in layout and proof, to see that Shay has concentrated in pictures and text on bringing to you a clear, exciting photojournalistic record of how the winners win—or how they think they do.

I should confess at the outset to a prejudice. I liked Art Shay the first day we met. He had come to photograph me for *Sports Illustrated* and we ended up playing handball together. As the official photographer for both racquetball and handball, Art has been one of the mainstays in the growth of both sports. His collaborator in *Winning Racquetball*, young Chuck Leve, doesn't need an introduction around the world of racquetball. As National Director of the U.S. Racquetball Association and editor of *National Racquetball Magazine* and a friend of most of the top pros—despite being the game's best referee—Chuck's guiding hand is visible on every spread.

Like the racquetball pros, Shay behind his four-frame-a-second camera is a fierce competitor. His concentration behind the telephoto lens during a match is worth looking away from the court to see. Pro Commissioner Joe Ardito and I stood on the sidelines as Art and Chuck polished their interviews and layouts. There are other books on racquetball, and they are uniformly useful for beginners. But this is the only book I have personally endorsed.

If you are a good racquetball player—and want to move ahead to "winning racquetball"—this is the book for you.

Bob Kendler
President, U.S. Racquetball Association
President, U.S. Handball Association

# acknowledgments

Having covered sports as a photographer for *Sports Illustrated* for some fifteen years, I have had many opportunities to work with professionals in almost all sports. No single group of pros I ever met surpasses the small fraternity of pro racquetballers as sportsmen, gentlemen, and teachers. Chuck Leve and I would like to thank these exemplary people: Charlie Brumfield, Steve Keeley, Steve Serot, Charlie Drake, Marty Hogan, Bill Schmidtke, and others for their help.

Many thanks also to my son and photographic assistant, Dick Shay, who took many of the photographs in this book, my favorite being the victory picture on the last page. And thanks, too, to Astra Photo Service in Chicago for their fine processing.

Arthur Shay
Deerfield, Ill.

# chapter one

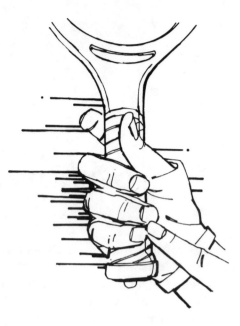

# the ball,
# the racquet, the grip

Our assumption is that you have been playing racquetball for some time. You have perhaps progressed from the pickup game to the rigorously scheduled one or two hours a week at your latest friendly "Court House," "Supreme Court," or those six or eight tempting white courts so casually set in behind all those busy tennis courts.

Possibly from tennis, perhaps a bit from handball, maybe even from that general aura of fair-to-average shape that surrounds "doers" of sports rather than TV "watchers," you really powder the ball. You can run hard without exhaustion, retrieve fairly well, and as noted, hit hard. But you *lose* too often. You make too many technical errors —bobbles that cost you points. You seem to be floundering around without making much progress. Fun is fun, but winning is better, right?

OK. This book is for you.

Racquetball's Babe Ruth, Charlie Brumfield, lines up a forehand kill.

Flying through the air, as he often does, doesn't help Steve Serot in this case.

We assume that you are properly outfitted in shorts and shirt or blouse. Your sneakers have good tread. There's nothing wrong with your tennis clothes as long as they don't bind.

If you perspire a lot you might add headband and wristband. Several companies now make good racquetball gloves. Some players use handball gloves, others use the new paddle tennis gloves.

As for eyeguards, either aluminum tubing with no lenses or regular athletic glasses with your prescription are highly recommended by the dozen pros we've interviewed for this book. Alas, they do not all wear them in competition. All-time great Charlie Brumfield says, "Pros have less chance of hurting each other because they generally have

3

The "green" and the "black"— racquetball's two most popular balls.

more control and know pretty much where they're hitting and where their opponents are.''

So start out right, with an eyeguard of some kind, even if it's only a pair of tempered prescription glasses with strong frames.

## THE BALL

There are several good brands of racquetball on the market. (The most popular is the Seamco.) The regulation ball is 2.5 inches in diameter, weighs 1.4 ounces, and will bounce about six feet when dropped from an arm-extended overhead position. (See the Appendix for more specific information about the regulation tournament ball.)

## THE RACQUET

There are two types of racquet head shapes—the teardrop design

Whether the racquet you buy is owl-faced, long-faced, metal, wood, glass-filled, or composite, racquet choice is an individual, experimental activity. Note Brumfield's comments on stringing tension in the text.

and the owl's-head design. Racquetball's Babe Ruth, Charlie Brumfield (still very active in championship pro play at 27), prefers the owl's-head design, which is narrower than the teardrop, but of course more circular.

Brumfield, the game's foremost and most explicit theoretician as well as best player, feels that on hitting any shot with less than perfect contact between ball and racquet—in short, most shots for most players—the narrower-faced round racquet tends to "reduce the racquet twisting in your hand."

Many former tennis players might find the transition to a tear-shaped racquet easier, as another perennial champ, Steve Strandemo, does. Says Strandemo, "A lot depends on what you get used to."

Brumfield agrees. He began playing with a basic Ektelon racquet and accustomed his game to the circular head because he "liked the hitting area." (Of course, Brumfield and Strandemo could use Ping-

Pong paddles and still beat 80 percent of all racquetball players alive!)

Racquetball pros like to talk of flexibility in their racquets. They feel that relative flexibility is the primary difference between metal and fiber-filled composite racquets. The fiber-fills, which are having their day in tennis, are more flexible, in general, than metal. Brumfield feels that fiber-fill helps enhance his control, enabling him to wait until the last split second to commit his shot. "In addition," he says, "it helps me use a softer swing much of the time, so I don't have to power the ball each time." He does allow, however, getting into way-out theory (where he is at home), that "the disadvantage of the flexible racquet lies in its very flexibility. Because of the flexibility, the hitting zone at the top of the racquet is inferior to that of a metal racquet; however, the edge response is not as good."

If you're a heavy-handed slugger, start out with a metal racquet.

A second disadvantage of the composite racquet, some pros feel, is its lack of durability. Racquet for racquet, they feel, a well-made metal racquet is simply more durable than the fiber-fill composite type.

You must, therefore, try to play with a few different racquets before deciding on one. It's a matter of feel. If you feel that your game is going to progress along the lines of control—like Brumfield's or Steve Keeley's game—you want flexibility in a racquet. Ektelon has done a lot of work milling their racquet heads of metal to try to achieve the same flexibility you can get out of a fiber-filled racquet. Leach and Vittert are both doing research in this way-out field of racquet design. As the sport continues its fantastic growth, the average player eyeing a higher level of play will be the beneficiary of the money and research devoted to his primary weapon.

Brumfield notes that if you want to play a hard-driving game and are basically a heavy-handed slugger who loves to take his aggressions out on the innocent ball, then metal is probably the place for you to start. Most of the game's pros who are hard hitters started with metal. Strandemo says, "Metal makes the ball leave the racquet instantly. This gives you a more accurate response in a hard hit."

This is the same concept that golfers use. A Jack Nicklaus uses a stiff shaft because with all his power he's got to have control. As a winning racquetball player, you're going to want some of that same control.

## Stringing Along to the Sweet Spot

At the Brumfield-Strandemo-Nicklaus level of play, no aspect of a sport is unimportant.

So far we've been talking about the flexibility of racquet *frames*.

Both Strandemo and Brumfield allow that a shot coming off the perimeter of a metal racquet is a "little" more accurate. (In Birdie Tebbetts' classic comment, "Baseball is a game of inches"; so, too, is racquetball. "The hardest thing to call in racquetball," says co-author and veteran referee Chuck Leve, "is the skip or no-skip kill shot. Did it graze the floor by a split fraction of an inch or didn't it?")

To Strandemo and Brumfield, that "little" means lots of points.

Fiberglass racquets, it is alleged by the pros, have a "sweet spot."

7

The ball stays on the strings for an added split second, so if 'hit properly the shot comes off the strings with a high degree of control and power. "It's like hitting a tennis shot right," says Strandemo. "You'll soon come to feel the sweet spot. Ektelon mills out a bit of each metal racquet head. It takes away a little strength, but it adds a little precision and accuracy. And the name of the game is accuracy."

Nearly everyone in racquetball has a different idea about the tension of strings on a racquet. The confusing factor, the pros feel, is that so many racquetball aficionados are former or current tennis players.

Good average tennis-racket tension is around 50 to 55 pounds. Brumfield plays racquetball at a string tension of *18!* This is well below the figure at which most manufacturers send their racquets from the plant. Why? Brumfield's theory is that the average racquet buyer is a tire-kicker type of shopper. If the strings feel "loose," the buyer will think it's shoddy merchandise.

Before loosening your racquet down to Brumfield's playing tension, he recommends that average players with fiber-fill racquets play at about 25 to 28 pounds. Metal racquets, 30 to 32 pounds. (The stiffer the tension, the quicker the departure of ball from racquet, but with a slight loss of control. Compromises, compromises!)

If you have ever played paddle tennis you will realize that the strings work harder for you than wood. The tighter a racquet is strung, the closer the strings come to providing a woodlike response.

The answer is to learn by feel and experience and experiment—as in all other good systems of learning.

If you suspect your stringer is lacing your racquet too tightly, Strandemo recommends getting a new stringer, educating your old one, or "just put it in with your wet gym clothes for a week to loosen up."

## Grip and Gloves

There are two basic materials used on a racquet grip—leather and rubber. Most pros have experimented with both.

The advantage of the rubber grip is durability. You can wash it every two weeks and keep it feeling new. Rubber slips a bit more than leather, but it's more durable. Leather just wears away. Slippage

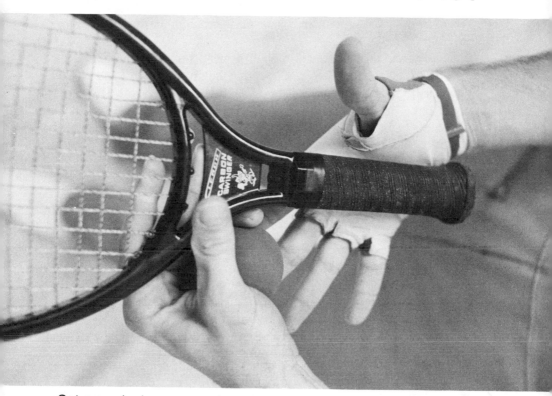

Get a good grip on your grip and you're on your way to a basic grasp of racquetball.

comes from accumulated perspiration—the salt, mostly, that builds up. Soap and water washes it away.

Most pros wash and dry their hands and their racquet handles between games to diminish the slippage—even with leather gloves. Leather gloves are used by nearly all of the pros. "You can't pick up a dime from the floor with a glove," Brumfield admits. "So you lose a bit of sensitivity. But the key concept is to make the racquet an extension of your hand. I play with a glove in which I've cut out the fingers. So I regain a bit of that lost sensitivity. The major sweat areas are still covered by the glove." Brumfield cuts his own gloves because he finds that the half-finger gloves on the market are generally too long. He

9

recommends Champion and Saranac—although he has no contract with either.

Gloves should be cleaned in warm water with soap—no hard detergents. And wash them by hand. As they begin to dry, fit them on your hand and rub and flex the leather so that the gloves are soft. If you play with three or four pairs of gloves and keep changing the bands and washing the gloves, you will extend the life of the gloves considerably.

## Grip Size

Many players coming to racquetball from tennis are used to a relatively large diameter grip. A large grip, most pros feel, is incorrect for racquetball because racquetball makes more extensive use of the wrist than does tennis. The actual purpose of the large tennis grip is to restrict the amount of wrist that enters a swing. A larger grip helps you keep your wrist locked. The checkpoint of the proper racquetball-sized grip is when your hand surrounds the racquet, the fingers should almost be able to touch the meaty portion of your palm.

Women especially should be very careful about getting a racquet with a grip that's too thick. An improper match of grip size to player's hand can result in *a loss of 50 percent of your hitting power!*

## Gripping the Racquet—Brumfield's Way

The one fundamental most beginning racquetball players have trouble with is seemingly the simplest: how to hold the racquet. "I can almost guarantee that no one at this seminar knows how to hold the racquet properly," Brumfield told a group of 100 advanced players recently gathered for the New England Open in Burlington, Vermont. The few snickers turned into frozen grins after Brumfield held forth on the grip for a while.

1. The racquet head has to be an extension of your hand and you can't manage this without the proper grip.

2. The objective of the grip is to hold the racquet in such a way that when we enter the proper hitting zone, the racquet face is *square to the intended line of flight of the ball.*

10

Brumfield recommends a slight "choke" on the racquet. Emphasis should be on the last three fingers of the gripping hand.

3. When you hit the ball, you want the racquet face pointed toward the target—the spot on the side wall, front wall, or ceiling you're aiming for. Not inclined down, bent up, or twisted sideways. We want square impact on forehand and backhand.

4. This square impact makes it easier for you to aim the ball at your target. Secondly, a square racquet face lets you get maximum power out of your swing—because any tilt cuts the percentage of power by the percentage of the tilt. You can hire a mathematician, physicist, or computer to work this out—or practice until you feel it yourself. You will gradually feel your power grow as you make your swing squarer.

5. It will come as a surprise to many that you can't get a square

11

impact with the same grip on both sides, forehand and backhand.

6. The forehand grip is achieved in this way: Hold the racquet in your off hand and put your playing hand over the face of the string. Now move this hand down the face of the racquet until you are midway down the grip. Now shake hands with the racquet.

7. Shaking hands this way, you'll notice that you've choked up slightly on the butt of the racquet. This merely helps make the racquet an extension of the hand. Of course, there are many players who *don't* choke up on their racquets, but Brumfield, the grip-master, feels that they play well in spite of their grips, not because of them.

8. The opposite theory is that if you move your hand down lower on the racquet, your arc of swing is going to be longer and you're going to hit the ball harder. Theoretically, that's true. In practice, however, Brumfield feels that racquetball is a rapid-fire sport that requires square contact in order to generate maximum racquet-head speed, and that in 11 years of competitive play he's concluded that you make best contact with the ball with your full hand on the racquet and choked up slightly —from three-quarters of an inch to an inch.

He recommends a simple experiment for doubters. Hold the racquet in a down position. Waggle it. Try to get the feel of how much control you have over the club head. Now move your hand up to the face of the racquet and perform the same experiment. You'll probably feel a sense of solidarity between the club head and your hand.

9. Do not hold the racquet as you would a baseball in your palm. Do not use the "fist grip." The goal in racquet gripping is a concept equal to the tennis concept of *finger spread*. The emphasis on the grip should be *on the last three fingers of your playing hand*. Don't pinch with your thumb and forefinger. Hang loose. If you apply too much pressure with thumb and forefinger, that amounts to a freezing of the muscles in your arm. Did you ever see a well-muscled football player try to play racquetball? His motion usually lacks fluidity. It's a matter of fusing your entire set of hand and arm muscles and keeping them fluid and supple at the same time. If you pinch with these muscles you can't generate power. You end up muscling the ball instead of swinging at it.

Brumfield's idea of a totally fluid swing is young Marty Hogan's. Hogan's idea of a great swing is Charlie Brumfield's! Both are fluid as

12

It is impossible to overemphasize the importance of meeting the ball with the racquet square to it.

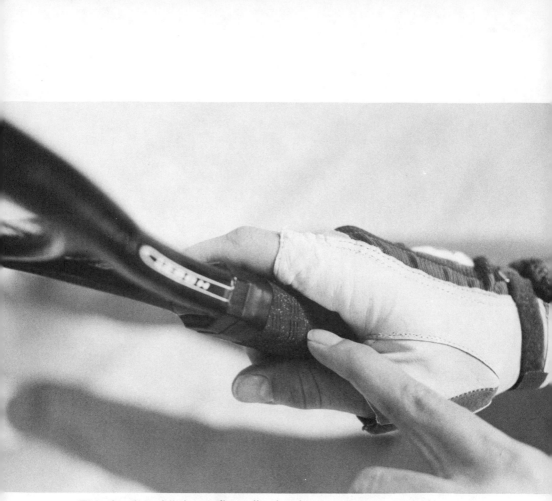

This forehand "trigger finger" grip gives you more control.

can be, and illustrate the seeming miracle of the 130-pound golfer, like Ben Hogan (no relation to Marty), who could power the ball 270 yards at will. Racquetball is truly one of those sports in which "getting it all together" is more than a hip idiom. It's the secret known to all great "hitters" in all sports involving the smooth transfer of power from athlete to object.

10. Brumfield favors the "trigger-finger grip." The trigger finger is extended up the handle, beyond the other fingers, for control. The "feel" of the grip should be in the fingers, not the palm. "It's the same concept as shooting a basketball," Brumfield teaches. "The coach tells you to shoot off your fingertips and not to rest the ball in

your palm. The fingers, you should remember, are more sensitive, and you're working for control. Control comes from the *fingers!*"

11. The final part of the racquetball grip for the forehand is to determine for yourself whether or not the grip is too far to the right or the left. This determination is made by imagining the letter "V" formed by your thumb and forefinger. The point of that "V" should go right up the middle of the racquet in the forehand grip.

12. If your grip at this point does all of the things discussed above, then when you move the racquet into the hitting area that racquet face is *square*—and square is the name of the game.

Brumfield ardently feels that "any other grip is just not right. The most personal thing about your game," he continues, "is your grip. People are always asking me whether it's worth changing their grip to improve their play. I always answer this by saying there's no answer to anyone who doesn't have the consciousness to make the grip change and learn how to hold the racquet properly. These people who can't change can still play racquetball, and possibly have fun with it—but their play will always be at a very low level. The essence and the real fun of this game, I feel, is to improve in it—to play winning racquetball. This involves building your game to achieve your maximum potential."

## The Backhand (Preliminary Discussion)

1. Remember the objective: to have the racquet face enter the hitting zone and line of flight of the ball *square*.

2. Using your forehand grip, as developed above, try swinging backhanded. The racquet inclines, right? It's pointed upward. This inclination is responsible for about a third of all bad racquetball shots —this inability to change from a forehand to a backhand grip. Technically, what's happening is that the ball spins off the racquet face and floats to the front wall. It doesn't move solidly. It doesn't reflect the latent power in your arm and body.

3. What's the solution? Simple. Holding your racquet backhandedly, or in your "normal" backhanded position, turn the racquet in your hand until it reaches the square position. It's simple, but difficult to do because the ball may be coming at you at 100 mph. Now obviously

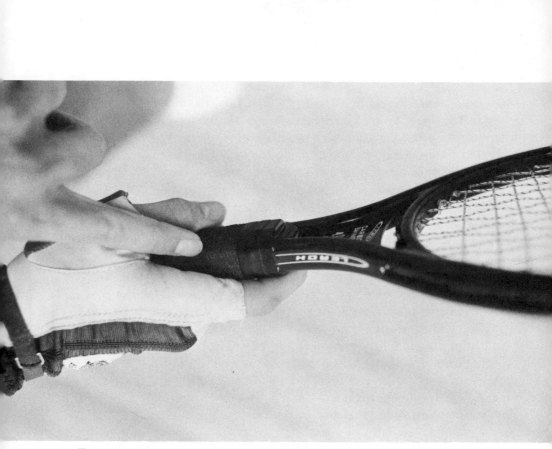

Try using your forehand grip on a backhand shot. It inclines, right? This inclination is responsible for about a third of all bad racquetball shots! This is a proper backhand grip. It's only a quarter of an inch of a turn!

you don't change your grip for every shot of the game. There are certain rapid-fire points up front where your grip remains the same. However, from backcourt or midcourt when you do have time, you should make the effort to change your grip until it comes naturally.

4. Pros such as Brumfield, Keeley, Hogan, and Serot hold their racquets in hand for three or four hours every day—so they know exactly where it is at every second. But you—on your way to winning racquetball—may have to use your opposite hand to steady the racquet as you make the change—and may even have to keep looking down to see that you're doing it right. When you see a pro looking down at his racquet after missing a shot, he is not merely angry, he is looking at his

16

If you're inclined to incline your racquet for backhand—don't.

grip or some other fundamental, wondering what caused him to miss, or better, trying to determine in a flash what it will take to correct the bobbled shot. No one wants to admit, even to himself, that he choked up mentally. So everyone, at that moment of truth after a bad shot, is hoping his or her grip was wrong. By all odds the grip is the most important of the fundamentals.

If you get nothing else from this book but an appreciation of the dynamics and importance of the grip, you will play better racquetball from the moment you hit the court with a better understanding of your basic grip—and how to make it *square*.

# chapter two

Before the actual swing itself, a player must "set up" for a shot; that is, get in position to hit the ball. For starters, most beginning players don't "carry" their racquets at a good ready position. Most carry it too low. This leaves a player ready for low shots but just a fraction behind time for arriving at a waist-high or ceiling shot. It is recommended that you carry your racquet waist-high. You're ready for anything above, below, or on line.

Without getting too deeply into foot position at this point, let it suffice to say that foot and racquet position are the keys to good shooting. Most players don't get far enough behind the ball when they shoot. Of course, good shoulder movement is important, too—everything is connected to that much-desired "fluidity" of motion mentioned above.

You must take or make the split second of time necessary to strike

# the swing

the ball properly—to bring your growing fluidity into action.

Exploding the moment of impact, and its predecessor moments, one would find the knees, hips, and shoulders coming in first—*just ahead of that square racquet*.

The swing, it should be emphasized, is much like the vaunted golf swing. Get that body, those arms, those legs, those shoulders—everything—into that moment of contact.

Beginners have trouble "getting behind" the ball. This is worth hours of practice—hours of chasing balls—just to get behind them and uncork a good swing. You should develop the knack of getting behind the ball, taking a natural step into it, getting all of your physical equipment into it, as dissected above. With practice this will soon come as naturally as rushing in and flailing away do now. One bonus

of racing to a position behind the ball is that with it comes the ability to retrieve shots that used to get away. This will involve snapping the wrist at the last moment—but if your feet have gotten you there, there's no reason why this shouldn't develop you as a great retriever. Naturally, this snapping maneuver is much harder to do on the backhand side—but it's the kind of stroke that pays off. Some pros will practice *one shot* 500 times and more at one session, until they feel they have it under control.

To sum up: In the racquetball swing, a player's objective should be to generate the greatest amount of power with the greatest amount of control. (Just as in life and business, come to think of it.) Almost anyone can be taught to hit a ball at 110 mph. The way to do it is to maximize the use of all parts of the body. Watch good quarterbacks. They set up well, weight comes off the back foot, everything aimed at the target. Or good golfers. If you don't "set up" properly, you'll strain your arm by not getting your weight—your body—into your shot. Recapitulating, let's break down the swing into departments:

1. First you get behind the ball and move your racquet to the ready position.

2. As soon as you determine you're going to swing a forehand shot you should automatically move your racquet into position at the top of the backswing—in other words, way back.

3. From there the only motion you need is forward movement.

4. Remember now, that the lower body is much stronger than the upper. Your power is largely in your buttocks, your back, and your legs. The buttocks and back are two fairly cumbersome components of your power base, so it takes some time to get the components all together into a developing swing. Take the time! Get behind that ball!

5. From your ready position you turn your hips, legs, and knees toward the target. This automatically lowers the racquet into a proper hitting position (assuming you've digested and applied the grip lesson).

6. Now comes the uncoiling of a previously coiled spring—the shoulders. Good shoulder movement will double the power of a swing.

7. A stop-motion picture of a good swing would show that *the arm*

(Facing page.) Brumfield "sets up" for a kill against Serot in classic form.

*does not move*. That's the key. To repeat: *The arm does not move.* Good leg and shoulder movement pulls the arm into the proper hitting position. If you move your arm early, you are doing what in golf is called "hitting from the top." If you hit from the top—in either golf or racquetball—your maximum club-head speed is reached too soon prior to the instant of contact. Thus you're hitting a weaker shot than you should with all that effort.

8. Driving the hips toward the target, channeling shoulders down and through—here is where you release your forearm or wrist and this is the best moment to contact the ball off the instep of your front foot. And then follow through straight up. Just like a golf shot! If you watch Jack Nicklaus or Johnny Miller, you will see this gigantic movement, the knees followed by the hips and shoulders, the wrists being released at last.

9. The chief fault of improper racquetball swinging is, alas, to swing

Even though Steve Keeley is strong, it is the fluidity of his motion that makes his technique masterful—not the muscle power.

like a tennis player. It involves using the shoulders but locking the arms. If your arms lock, you've cut half the power available to you. It must be hips, legs, forearms, shoulders, wrist—all working together.

The Master—Charlie Brumfield—says, "Here's how to prevent yourself from using a tennis swing. First, lead with your elbow. The elbow leads the swing in a proper racquetball swing, so the movement is this: drive; coil; elbow leads the racquet—and then you release. As long as your elbow stays ahead of the racquet, you've delayed that club face so that you can release at the last instant and generate that final 50 percent of the power you're looking for."

Watching Brumfield's—Serot's, Keeley's, Hogan's—gracefulness and fluidity and lots of victories underlines Brumfield's wise words: "We're looking for technique, not muscles, to produce power."

# chapter three

You now know how to hold the racquet properly—the complicated dynamics of which possibly shook you a little. As in all efforts toward self-improvement, nobody promises you a rose garden. It isn't easy. It isn't always fun. The fun lies in the achievement, in making a better player of yourself, in learning to win, win, win. On the positive side, *wanting* to win seems to be a fairly common human urge. The psychologists tell us that the popularity of *My Fair Lady* is due to our rooting for the common, garden-variety flower girl to improve her diction and style so that she can pass as a duchess—so she can *win*.

Kathy Williams, a highly successful Michigan pro who teaches a full schedule, strongly advises eager beginners who desire to advance to keep doing progressively more advanced racquetball drills and to supplement these with a constant harping on the basics.

# self-improvement

The hard-hitting Ms. Williams specializes in helping racquetballers who have practiced hard on their own and with friends for six months and at the end of that time are not much more proficient than they were at the outset. "In fact," she notes, "there are some touring racquetball pros who keep making the same basic-skill mistakes from year to year."

So you work hard on your fundamentals. Forehand, backhand, serve. What then?

Almost all of the pros, including Kathy, agree that you must make every effort to play better players than yourself and learn how your superiors handle certain shots and strategies. This will involve your attending tournaments—and the higher the caliber of competition, the better for you as a developing, improving player.

You must then try to get some feedback about how you're doing.

Hard-hitting pro Kathy Williams (left) practices what she preaches against high-ranked Jan Campbell.

Kathy recalls competing with another player for two years, during which her opponent never acquired a consistent kill. Kathy analyzed her difficulty as not letting the ball drop low enough toward the floor before hitting it. This player would instead try to kill from waist level. Talking to her, Kathy learned that her opponent *thought* she was hitting the ball "below knee level." A few practice sessions gave this player a much-improved kill shot.

Most of us are not totally aware of what our bodies are doing during action—we have a lack of "kinesthetic awareness." A player might *feel* that he or she is snapping the wrist properly at impact with the ball, when in fact the wrist is rigid as iron—and dissipating much of the body's power, to say nothing of accuracy.

Beginners should therefore practice in pairs so they can offer feedback to each other. Questions should accompany play. "Am I keeping my elbow close to my body during my swing?" "How high off the floor am I taking the shot?" "Am I shifting my weight to the front foot at contact?"

It doesn't take an expert to answer these questions. Moreover, it keeps you *thinking* about your fundamentals, about using them in the slow ascent of the ladder until they become second nature to you.

Here are some of the simple drills that Ms. Williams uses for beginners who are intent on improving:

1. *Drop and Kill:* This is probably the single most effective self-improvement exercise. Standing at midcourt and facing the side wall, drop the ball in front of the body at arm's length and stroke the ball to the front wall.

   A. Vary the height from the floor at which you hit the ball, working towards hitting it fairly close to the floor.
   B. Keep the elbow of the racquet arm close to the body.
   C. Step into the ball with the leg closest to the front wall, transferring the weight from the rear to the forward foot.
   D. Snap the wrist at the moment of contact.
   E. Rotate the hips and upper body toward the front wall.
   F. Try to feel the rhythm in the whole process, as in learning a dance step.

27

Fleet Jan Campbell momentarily uses the wall to balance herself for a retrieve.

**G.** Vary the speed of execution, so that your reflexes can adapt to slightly different situations within the same simple basic exercise. Remember—pros like Brumfield often try the same shot 500 times in one practice session!

2. *Back-Corner Pickup:* This drill is designed for players with little or no wrist snap and who have trouble digging the ball out of the back corners. Stand facing either back corner. Gently toss the ball into the corner so that it hits the back wall, side wall, and floor in that sequence. Start with a toss about four feet high and work down to one foot. At the one-foot level the only way the ball will get to the front wall is with a strong wrist snap. This wrist-snap motion should feel very much like the wrist does when you hit a nail with a hammer.

3. *Continuous Kill and Lob:* Start with a short soft lob to the front wall. Ideally the ball should bounce in the front part of

It's impossible to overemphasize the value of working on the fundamentals.

the court. After it bounces, try to kill the ball low to
the front wall. As it comes back after the kill (or miss!),
get your racquet under the ball and gently lob it back
again. Continue keeping the ball in play as long as you
can by alternating lobs and kills. This kind of contin
uous chase-the-ball play gives practice in kill shots
from all areas of the court, helps your footwork, and
gives you a good solo workout in a relatively short
time. It's also more fun than stopping the ball after
every kill, near-kill, or outright miss.

4. *Backhand versus Forehand:* If you have trouble, as most players
do, changing your grip from forehand to backhand, a
good additional exercise is playing them against each
other, shot for shot. It's a kind of positive paranoia
that will score points for you in competition—which
is the name of the game as well as the goal of this
book. What's more, if you're clumsy, you won't run
into anyone but yourself.

29

# chapter four

One of the best servers in the world, Steve Serot, puts it succinctly. "You score points when you have the serve—so that gives you an edge right away. You can score, and your opponent can't, when you serve. Don't forget, racquetball is a game of small edges, and serving is a pretty big edge. Next in importance is returning the serve. These are the two most basic shots in racquetball—as they are in tennis."

The best place to stand when serving is the middle of the serving area. Later on we will dwell on the wisdom of inhabiting the "center position" on the court—a kind of command-post area from which you can direct your game and often that of your opponent.

For the time being, let it suffice to say that the midcourt serving position is generally best for the server. It gives him or her a strategic base of operations. Remember, racquetball is a game of inches.

# the serve

To serve, you bounce the ball on the floor and hit it with your racquet toward any part of the front wall. The ball must go past the short line, of course, and land anywhere in the court. On its way it may hit either of the side walls. If it hits both side walls, that is a fault. If it hits the back wall before it hits the floor, that, too, is a fault or "long." (If it doesn't make it past the short line, the serve is a "short." Two shorts, or longs—or one of each—constitutes an *out,* also known as a *hand-out* —as in handing the ball over to your opponent so that he can serve.)

## DRIVE SERVE

The drive serve is the most frequently used serve. It is just a serve to

Pros such as Serot use the lob serve more often than one would expect.

Bill Schmidtke's drive serve is a much-feared weapon.

the wall that drives back in a straight line, usually near one of the side walls, without hitting it. When the ball lands low, just past the short line between floor and side wall, it is especially hard to return. This is a good serve if your opponent has been playing too far back. Similarly, a deeper drive serve will catch your opponent off balance if he has been playing too far forward. The back corner of the court is a particularly good target area for this serve.

33

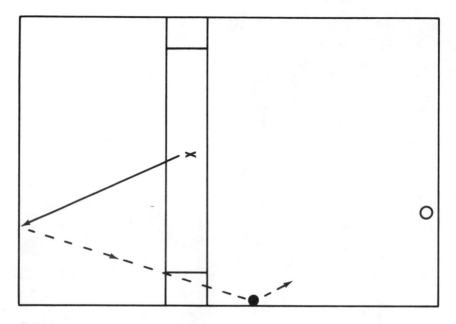

Drive serve.

The power and accuracy for the drive serve come from a good fore-hand stroke in which the ball is hit about knee-high and the body's weight shifts from back foot to front foot as you swing.

You must be careful with the drive serve, for if you miss the "crotch" of floor and wall or the back corner pocket, the serve will just hit the side or back wall and hang there for an easy kill by a competent opponent.

Many pros develop a stable of change-up speeds for the drive serve —from lightning-fast to slow-motion. The "off-speed" drive serve— about three-quarters of full power—is an effective variant, because it gives your opponent time to think of your strategy and how he's going to out-fox or out-psych you. This unnatural amount of thought often throws his return off a sufficient fraction to let a wily player capitalize on it.

(Some years ago, several of us who were serious handball players around the Evanston, Illinois, YMCA used to vie with each other for a

Steve Strandemo lobs a serve.

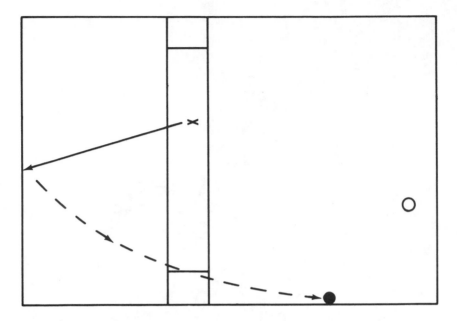

Lob serve.

chance to play against the Chicago Cubs pitcher Jim Brosnan or the Mets' Jay Hook. Why? Because big league pitchers *invented* the art of psyching opponents with changes of delivery and other tactics! If you could learn to fool one of *them,* you were on your way to more wins.)

## LOB SERVE

Most casual racquetball players watching a pro tournament are generally surprised at how many times the pros use the slow-speed lob serve as an offensive weapon. It is usually hit, by right-handed players, fairly high on the front wall, or high enough so that it hits the left wall about two strides from the rear wall. To serve left, your starting position is a little right of center. To serve to the left side, stand a little left of the center of the serving area. Ideally, this serve should peter out just as it hits the back wall—without your opponent's return. You must guard against your opponent's racing in and killing this serve on

36

the fly past you. You must especially make sure the serve doesn't make it to the back wall, bouncing off to give your opponent an easy kill at worst, or a setup at least. Deciding when to use the lob as a change-up is part of court strategy, about which more later. The instant decision to go to the lob also depends on how your opponent is playing —too far up, too far back—or seemingly tightly wound up and ready to return a hard-hit serve. The change-up will throw his entire response out of synchronization, often to your advantage.

As server, you should pick out the exact spot where you wish the serve to strike the front wall. You must remember, or learn, not to "push" your serve, but to strike the ball firmly and evenly. Gradually you will want to experiment with spin and speed change-ups.

Good lob serves hit the front wall, then strike the side wall high and deep, about seven or eight feet from the back wall. The natural spin on the ball, and the fact that it's a partial-speed shot, help this shot refrain from reaching the back wall with too much bounce left in it. If it does hit the back wall too fast, it comes off for an easy kill by your opponent. As noted, the ball will drop in or near the backhand corner without leaving the receiver-defender enough room to do anything but barely return the ball. Just because it's a "soft" shot, don't undersell the lob as an offensive or defensive weapon. Older players, especially, are well advised to develop a good "soft" game. A practiced soft-shot hitter can spot a much younger power hitter who isn't too accurate many points and many years. Slow lobs can also drive some power hitters absolutely ape with frustration. As in baseball, few home runs are hit off slow-ball pitches.

One thing that too many beginners and intermediate players neglect during the serving process is to know, each second, where your opponent is and where the ball is. This includes watching him or her retrieve the ball you've just served. Many players, for fear of being hit by the service return, turn away at this moment and have no idea where the ball is going until they see it come off the front wall. This is a vital, fundamental part of winning racquetball. After serving the ball, you should peep over your shoulder (left shoulder if the serve was left, right shoulder if it went right) to watch your opponent. You should not serve, then stand there looking dead ahead. You lose perhaps a full

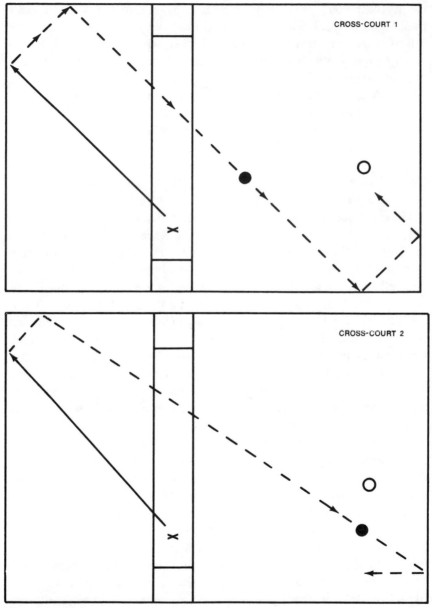

Cross-court serve.

two steps in your brain's early-warning-system operation. Watch good tournament players. They seem to know exactly where the ball is coming from. That "knowing" is no secret instinct—just good reflexes—and the ability to read your opponent's body motions. Anticipation is what you're after.

Serving is an advantage, as we've said. But it's up to you to keep your advantage, and to build on it. Anticipation—and those quick glances in which you "read" your opponent—are the key.

## CROSS-COURT SERVE

To serve cross-court, you use a forehand swing, making the ball hit about three feet from the junction of front wall and side wall. The ball caroms sharply to the opposite side wall, and if it isn't retrieved in midflight, will strike the rear wall. Ideally this serve has formed the letter "Z"—which gives it one of its other names, the "Z serve." It is also called the "scotch serve" for reasons that vary from the origin of the player who first used it, to the sharpness of its function.

A variant of the cross-court serve calls for you to hit the ball closer —around two feet—to the junction of front wall and right side wall. The ball comes back to the rear wall without hitting that left side wall deep. This is a good serve to a right-handed opponent with a weak backhand.

Varying speed and height in the two cross-court serves just mentioned will give you an arsenal of offensive weapons to use strategically. It goes without saying—or nearly without saying—that when using the cross-court serve, care should be exercised against hitting the side wall or ceiling before hitting the front wall. If this happens, it's an automatic out for you. This is called a *non-front serve*. If you hit this serve too hard and without proper accuracy, you risk a *three-wall serve,* giving you a *fault*. Two faults and you're out.

## REVERSE CROSS-COURT SERVE (THE "GARFINKEL" OR "GARBAGE" SERVE)

Charlie Garfinkel was and still is a competitive racquetball player who first popularized a version of the reverse cross-court serve that

39

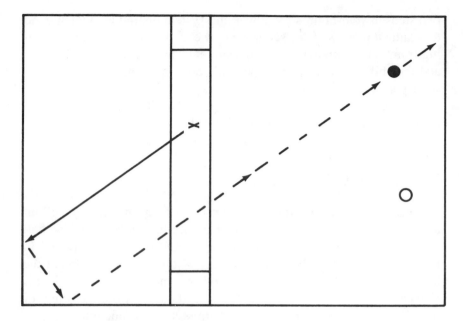

Reverse cross-court serve.

came to bear his name. It is a bold serve, for it involves hitting to an opponent's strong-hand side—to his or her strength. You serve at medium speed from a little right of center in the serving area. A forehand stroke sends the ball toward the left front wall, fairly close (within three feet) to the side wall. The ball caroms—front wall, side wall—and heads for the deep corner of the right back court—to your opponent's forehand.

As noted, this is a bold serve, and it will psych your opponent to the extent that he or she will be surprised that you have no respect for his/her strongest shot. This will often cut into your opponent's concentration and work towards a victory for you. A game of slight edges, remember?

An obvious advantage of any serve that comes into a deep corner is that your opponent will find it difficult to get his or her racquet behind the ball for an effective return or kill. A wobbly or soft return can give you a setup for a kill.

As in all serves, the risk of an inaccurate shot works to your oppo-

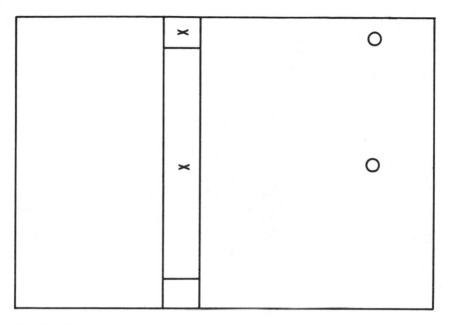

Serving in doubles.

nent's advantage. So practice hard on all your serves, especially one that seems to fit your style of play better than another.

As you move ahead into winning racquetball, you will learn how to gauge your opponent's wrist-snap, for example. If he or she can't snap that wrist quickly, then serving to both deep corners with any of the serves or variations will score points for you.

The point about the deep corners can't be overstressed. Most players need a certain amount of room in which to get their racquets behind the ball for a return. The more accurately you hit these corners, the less room you allow your opponent for killing against you.

## DOUBLES SERVING

When two right-handed players play as a team, the one with the better backhand should play the left side. There is much argument about whether a right- and a left-handed player make the best *theoreti-*

41

Drive serves and cross-courts are more effective than lobs in doubles.

*cal* team. "What about the center?" one asks. Some players, regardless of handedness. take to one side or the other in doubles play, as in tennis or handball. Only experiment and practice will reveal which arrangement works best for you and your partner.

The basic doubles serve has the server in the service zone and his partner in the service box with his back to the wall. He can't leave the service box until his partner's serve has passed the short line.

Drive serves and cross-court serves are more effective in doubles play than are the lobs.

If you and your partner are determined to play winning racquetball, this is probably the place to quote U.S. Handball Association secretary Mort Leve. "There is correctness, honesty, and sportsmanship in doubles play in handball and racquetball. But the courtesy of alternating serves to one opponent and then the next is out. That's OK for club play—but in serious competition, you pick out the weaker opponent, probe for his or her weakest spot, and you and your partner keep banging away at that spot while it produces points." (See rule 4.2.)

Alas, it's one of those cases in which nice guys finish last. If this causes a problem for you, you'd better content yourself with club and singles play—or pick up some guidance from quarterbacks, who keep probing for the weak spots in their opponents' defenses.

If you're on the embarrassing receiving end of this kind of serving, it should spur you to practice serve returns until you are no longer an easy mark.

# chapter five

The serve return is a defensive shot that a good player can turn into an offensive shot by placing it properly. Nothing short of a long rally is more exciting to watch in any court sport than the nearly perfect ace of a serve converted by a great save-return into a kill shot by the defender. Serot, Keeley, Brumfield, and Hogan are all masters of this—as is Jimmy Connors in tennis.

There are six principal serve returns: the drive, ceiling, kill, lob, Z-ball, and around-the-wall ball. Each has its primary and basic function (see below). As with most racquetball shots, service returns can be either forehanded or backhanded. Since almost 90 percent of all serves made in tournament play are to the receiver's backhand, you should spend more time and effort on executing service returns with your backhand than with your forehand.

# return of serve

The server has watched you practice or play, and now comes at you with a cross-court, Garfinkel, or lob. Your task is to hit the ball—either on the fly, before it bounces, or after one bounce—and get it back to the front wall. Simple. Most players choose to return the ball to the front wall via a side wall or two and/or the ceiling. This gives you time to get set for your next shot—and also time to retrieve a position in the center of the court—a sort of central command position—about which more later.

If you're fairly new to the sport, this is the time to make all those fundamental decisions about forehand, backhand, grip, etc. If you read the rules (see Appendix) you will see that changing the racquet from right hand to left in midplay is a no-no. You may be the rare player who can develop a two-handed grip, as some tennis players do. But by and

45

Fleet Dave
Bledsoe makes
a sensational
return, killing
against Brumfield.

large you will succeed best by using your orthodox forehand and back-hand against a serve that more often than not comes to your backhand.

## RETURNING THE DRIVE SERVE

A drive serve usually comes at you quickly. Returning it, you should hit just as hard. The advantage of the speed coming at you will then work for you, and you should be able to get the ball past your opponent before he or she can get set for a return of your return. Here is your opportunity to control the tempo of the game. If your opponent has been hitting high-arcing lobs or slow drives, a screamingly hard return by you will change this tempo to one that suits your game. Initiative has all sorts of tactical and psychological advantages if you take it.

There are two basic drive returns you can use for returning serves: The *down-the-line drive return* and the *cross-court drive return*. For the down-the-line return, usually a backhanded shot, your goal is to

Racquetball's Mickey Mantle, Marty Hogan, plays a down-the-line drive return against Rich Wagner.

powder the ball right down the left wall, as close to it as possible without touching it. Theoretically it should die in the left rear corner, impossible for your opponent to retrieve.

But perfection is rare, so it's a good idea to keep this return from hitting the wall, if possible. If it hits, it can pop out and give your opponent an easy return.

The other drive return favored by the pros is a cross-court. But this shot has to be chosen carefully. It works best when your opponent is *not* near center court and thus in position to intercept and kill your return.

OK. You swing your backhand hard at the ball, to make it hit the front wall to the right of center and go back to the deep right-hand corner. (Lefties please reverse the whole plan.) Drive returns are generally most effective when hit fairly low and fast. Surprise will work for you along with the speed. But mostly, by now, you should be thinking ahead, of the kind of shot you'll be offering your opponent if your drive isn't absolutely perfect. This thinking ahead is an important

47

part of winning racquetball. Willie Mosconi, the great pocket billiards player, once told me he invariably thinks four to six shots ahead, allowing for alternate returns by his opponent!

## CEILING RETURNS

When the good tournament player feels he can't kill the serve coming to him, no matter what kind it is, he invariably goes to his favorite playing surface—the ceiling. The most effective ceiling shots seem to be fairly hard-hit balls hitting the ceiling about two to four feet from the front wall, rebounding to the front wall, hitting the floor in the serving area, then ending up dying in one of the back corners. A good ceiling return gives your opponent very little to shoot at. This is why some tournament matches seem to be endless ceiling shots countered by other ceiling shots. Great care must be exercised that these shots make it all the way back—otherwise they hang up in midcourt and give your opponent some easy kills.

The popularity of the ceiling ball began with the arrival of Seamco's lively ball. For most racquetballers the backhand ceiling return is more difficult than the forehand. Thus, your ceiling ball should ideally cling to the side wall as it loafs toward the backhand corner. (A ball that stays right on or next to the side wall going down the line is called a "wallpaper ball.")

## THE KILL RETURN

The kill return, when it works, is the most effective shot there is. Like the home run, the hole-in-one, the hockey goal slap-shot, it's what the game is all about—winning.

A kill is a return that strikes the front wall so low that it is impossible for your opponent to retrieve. The ultimate in kill shots is called the "flat roll-out"—a shot that hits the wall so low that it rolls away from

(Facing page.) Steve Strandemo and Bill Schmidtke sometimes go to the ceiling for ten shots in a row before trying a kill.

the front wall with no bounce at all, just a happy or sickening thud—depending on whether you made the shot or it was made against you.

A near-miss kill of this kind is called a ''skip-in,'' ''skip-ball,'' or just plain ''skip.'' These misses are sometimes so close and hard to see that referees rely on their ears more than their eyes to call this one. A microsecond before the ball reaches the wall in a ''skip,'' you can hear the ''kiss'' or ''hiss'' of the ball scraping the floor on its way in. Many of the classic arguments among players, and with referees, involve interpretations of ''skip'' balls.

Technically, the kill return can be hit successfully off any poorly executed serve—or good one, for that matter. The percentages of completion lie with hitting the poor serve. The ''easiest'' kind of shot to kill is a ball off the back wall. Charlie Brumfield estimates that he attempts one kill attempt out of every ten balls served to him ''just to keep 'em guessing.''

Of course, the trick, even in killing, is to allow yourself a Plan B if your miss is not a ''skip'' or other out.

The kill return is, percentage-wise, not a very prudent shot—unless you've practiced it for long hours. But when it's done right, you know that you're learning the game, and its psychological boost is gratifying.

## THE LOB RETURN

The advent of the live ball in 1971 has seen the lob drop in popularity, giving way to the ceiling ball. In the early years of racquetball, the successful player could not survive without a lob. Now—although many good club players, especially older ones, use it—it is used mostly as a service return. Almost all good lobs are down-the-wall shots, defensive maneuvers. ''When I can't do anything else,'' says perennial champion Charlie Brumfield, ''I'll lob.'' The lob can be hit in return of any serve. The ideal lob is a ball hit at slow speed. It lazily hits the front wall high and, without touching the ceiling, glides down the line, touching the side wall at about three-quarters court. It then caroms into the deep back corner. As with the lob serve, if the ball does not strike that side wall, it will come off the back wall with sufficient speed to give your opponent a setup.

50

Keeping the lob off the back wall and away from the ceiling is very difficult to do with the live ball. So practice it if it suits your developing style of play.

# THE Z-BALL RETURN

The Z-ball return, properly executed, is one of the most effective service returns. It is also the most difficult—after the kill—to hit correctly. It requires a good deal of strength and pin-point accuracy. The chance of error is quite high in this shot—and error can lead to disaster if your opponent is alert. Think letter "Z"!

Now that you're properly frightened, let's examine the shot. It can be hit either forehand or backhand. The Z-ball return is hit similarly to the scotch serve in that it catches the front wall near the crotch of the side wall. The Z-ball, though, must be hit hard enough and high enough to carom from the front wall to the side wall, then travel across the court to the other side wall. In doing so it shouldn't hit the ceiling—for that would absorb the spin and speed of the shot, making the ball drop in midcourt for a potential kill by your opponent. The correctly hit Z-ball will carom off the last side wall it hits so close to the back wall as to make an effective return almost impossible.

# AROUND THE WALL RETURN

The around-the-wall return is something like the Z-ball return, but has the virtue of being easier to hit. It is stroked the same, but must hit the side wall *before* it hits the front wall. Thus the shot goes: side wall, front wall, then side wall again, a little past midcourt. Properly placed, this shot will move toward the rear wall and force your opponent from the all-important center-court position (see below)—which you can then commandeer as a game-control center.

# DOUBLES SERVE RETURN

Having studied your opponents in warm-up or in previous matches,

51

Steve Keeley's speed and lightning coordination make it possible for him to make "impossible" retrieves and returns.

you know something of their weaknesses. Is his backhand creaky? Serve to it. Does the team get mixed up in center court? Zip the ball between them. And so on. Generally, the ceiling ball return or Z-ball return is a good doubles return. Trying for kills in doubles is especially risky, for the rate of error is high, as is the number of times your opponents are left with easy shots.

On service returns, don't step into the serving area as you return a short serve, or rush in to retrieve a crotch serve near the serving line. If you step into the serving zone, you'll lose a point. Study the rules. Receiver must stand at least five feet behind the short line and not return the ball until it passes the short line. Don't touch the ball, even on an obvious out, until it hits the floor twice. You could have a *hinder* called against you, costing you a sure point.

As a receiver you should remember that this moment of truth is the most difficult you will be in for the entire rally; the advantage and the odds are with the server, as it is in almost any sport that has a serve. So practicing effective service returns is a rewarding expenditure of time. If you can't get a partner to serve practice shots at you, do it yourself. Just plan your practice session to include the weak spots in your game and work on them. Just because something is obvious doesn't mean that it's wrong or not worth doing. Concentrate. Anticipate. Admittedly you'll have a little trouble looking over your shoulder after you serve—to watch yourself return your own serve—but in a paranoid world it's calming to remember one of Freud's definitions of sanity: Holding two conflicting ideas and yet continuing to function.

# chapter six

Steve Strandemo is one of the top half dozen racquetball players in the country and a fine theorist. Watching him play is like watching an instructional movie. He has a secret that goes beyond the classic advice of "Practice, practice, practice, and keep playing players who are better than you." Here is his secret, courtesy of *National Racquetball Magazine:*

To win consistently in racquetball, center-court position must be attained and retained throughout the match. It is the command-post position. It is the best strategic position on the court for all-around operations. From this position you are able to control the play, choose from a wide selection of shots, and cover your opponent's shots. All this can be done better from center court than from any other location. For the record, center-court position is midway between the side walls about one step past the short line. This puts you equidistant from the

# center-court position—key to winning racquetball

crucial court zones surrounding you, and you will have a better chance of retrieving your opponent's shots—*on the percentage basis*—than you would have from any other position.

Midcourt position gives you enough swinging and retrieval room to kill into corners, kill balls on the fly, hit cross-court or down-the-line wallpaper balls, ceiling or Z-ball shots. Think of midcourt position as a kind of operations base from which you can get anywhere you want to go with the greatest efficiency, on the average, taking into account all balls that come to you during a match. Almost every shot in racquetball except the backwall shot can be handled from center court.

To repeat, the smart player will use this position as his headquarters, keeping his opponent off balance and retrieving while he conserves his own strength and waits for a mistake he can kill.

The overall strategy of a racquetball player should be carried in the mind as a background for every maneuver. If that strategy is to maintain center-court position as much as possible, that idea should always motivate—or partly motivate—every court action.

OK. How do we attain center-court position? The easiest method of taking control of center court is to win the previous point. By gaining the serve you have automatically put yourself in control of the center court at the outset of the next rally. The best way not to lose it is to concentrate on a strong, effective serve, causing a weak return by your opponent.

To play winning racquetball you must learn to vary your serve to keep your opponent guessing and to capitalize on any weakness in him or her that you have noticed. Usually the backhand is a good place to start probing for weaknesses, using various serves until you find a weakness. Change speeds, try cross-court serves, and mix in a lob or two.

Now you have moved from merely serving to serving with a couple of purposes: holding center-court position and determining opponent weakness so that the principal objective—aside from winning, or along with winning—can be reached. Do not fall into the habit of serving the same way and to the same place each time. This will enable your opponent to get set, to anticipate your serve, and to hit an effective return. Worse, it will allow him or her to gain that precious center-court position. Whoever controls the center court controls, and usually wins, the game. So let it be *you* in the driver's seat!

But what if you're not serving? How do you regain center court? As receiver, all percentages are against you. First, the server, as pointed out above, has a multitude of possible serves he can throw at you. Secondly, even if the server should hit you a poor serve, you still have to return it effectively just to regain the serve. But if you should hit a poor shot, chances are you will lose a point. That's the bad news.

So what do you do? We have already discussed the various serve returns as technical maneuvers. Let's now look at them in terms of overall center-court strategy—the four primary serve returns that will help you retrieve center-court position.

(Facing page.) Theoretician Steve Strandemo says the maintenance of the center-court position is the key to winning racquetball—and he's a winner.

The first, if it works for you, is the best. The kill shot return enables you to regain the serve immediately. Since a high percentage of serves (around 90 percent in tournament play) will come to your backhand, the best place to shoot-to-kill is into the front left corner (assuming you are in the group of six out of seven players who are right-handed). This shot should be attempted only when you have a complete setup—that is, your opponent's serve comes in slightly off, giving you enough room and time to hit your shot properly. Remember, however, that the kill return is the most dangerous of returns, for if your shot is too low it will hit the floor in a "skip," resulting in a point for your opponent.

The second return, and that used most often by good players, is the ceiling return. This shot allows you some margin for error, and when executed properly *will drive your opponent out of center court* to chase the ball. It will also make it extremely difficult to hit an offensive shot against you. About the best thing he can do is return another ceiling ball.

Against a right-handed player, you should keep the ceiling return along the left side wall, his or her backhand side—striking the ceiling first about two to three feet before the front wall. It will then hit the front wall on a good downward path, bounce on the floor, and rebound into deep left court along the wall.

Have patience! Prolong the ceiling rally until your opponent makes a mistake. Then move in and capitalize on it—*and retrieve that center-court position. That is your headquarters and you shouldn't leave it for too long.*

The third option on serve return, and probably the easiest to hit, is the cross-court drive. In this case, hit the ball slightly to the right of center on the front wall, with enough force to drive the ball past the server. It is a good change-of-pace return, for most servers tend to lean toward the left side of the court. (A no-no for anyone intent on keeping center court!)

There are hazards, though, to the cross-court drive return. First, if your opponent is quick and anticipates the shot, it is easy for him to step into the cross-court lane, intercept the ball, and kill it into the

(Facing page.) Center court is just a step behind the short line, midway between the side walls.

right-hand corner. And since he is probably right-handed, this will be a forehand shot for him, making it that much easier. Second risk is if you hit the ball too hard, it will come off the back wall as a setup. Third, if you hit it too softly, it will rebound off the side wall for another forehand "plum" ball.

The fourth serve return would be a pass down the line on the left. This is a difficult shot to control, but very effective when hit properly. It is especially good when the server is creeping up toward that left corner. If you can "blow it by him" down the left wall, *you will force him to give up that center court.*

## DEFENSE

Now let's turn these situations around, as your opponent's serve comes to you. Assuming that your opponent is a center-court strategist, too—perhaps even having read these words—you must be ready to return the shots just discussed as well as hit them. This is what's known as court coverage, one of the keys to maintaining center-court position.

The absolute basic rule on all court coverage is KEEP YOUR EYE ON THE BALL AT ALL TIMES. Next to your racquet—maybe a little ahead of it—comes your eyes. Your eyes start all your systems going, so use them. Most of the "wood shots" and other misses come from taking the eyes from the ball for a split second. "This is the curse of the beginning handball player," says perennial handball champ Kenny Schneider. "Especially on shots coming off the back wall." And so it is in racquetball.

Moving into winning racquetball, you should by now be able to anticipate your opponent's shot to a certain extent. You remember to watch him over your shoulder as he gets set and swings. Remember, too, he has been running, hitting, changing directions, and is most likely somewhat fatigued. The more tired your opponent, the more likely he or she will fall into patterns of response that you can learn to read and capitalize on by showing up close to where the ball will be. Maintaining center-court position will help you do this and cut down your own fatigue. Center court is like the home keys on a typewriter.

Keeley's eye is on the ball as he paces it to the back wall. Handball great Paul Haber once declared, "I even watch the ball during time-outs!"

You can touch-type from other positions, but not as well as from the home keys.

When you retrieve the serve, do not drop back more than one or at the most two steps behind the short line. Now is the time for peeking over that left shoulder to get an indication of what type of return your opponent will hit. All you need is a short glance anyway, because you should have a pretty good idea of where the ball is coming from from the kind of serve you gave him. If you see him lean over for an attempted kill, begin to anticipate the shot and get set for it.

If he kills the ball flat, he'll of course win the rally, no matter if you're standing in that left corner with your racquet on the ground. So don't worry about it, because there's no defense against it. But if he fails to kill solidly (which happens most of the time) all you have to do is step in and re-kill his shot in that same left corner. Use a quick short stroke for speed and accuracy. By all means, in this situation, sacrifice power for accuracy. A left-wall, front-wall kill tight in the corner, or front-wall left-wall, is a high-percentage winner.

Obviously this re-kill will have a greater margin for error than your opponent's original kill attempt. Some of the good percentage working for you comes from the fact that you had to travel only from center court while he has to come in from deep left court to re-re-kill if he can.

If you are quick and have learned or are learning to anticipate, and your opponent has a tendency to attempt kills, you should risk giving him serves he will shoot. The percentages are all with you!

If your opponent drives you out of center court with a ceiling ball, there is very little you can do to regain center court other than hit another ceiling ball. He is in control. A kill attempt by you is a bad percentage shot; a Z-ball from deep left corner takes a Hercules to execute; a pass will not have enough steam on it, especially if you are along the left wall. Hit another ceiling ball and let him worry about it. Here is where your conditioning, practice, and court savvy will pay off.

To defense against the cross-court drive, try to anticipate the angle your opponent will use. This is not as difficult as it may sound, for there is only one path your opponent's shot can travel (if he executes correctly). That path is called the "passing lane." Since you are already in center court, this imaginary lane is limited for your opponent because you've eliminated the left side of the court. The extension of your arm and racquet, plus the one step you would take for any shot, cuts down another five feet. And if his shot hits the side wall before reaching deep court, it will carom into center court, where you already are, thus saving you another three feet against the wall. So now you see that the passing lane is down to two feet in width. You should be able to cover it.

When you get to the ball—you're on the right side now—use a short firm stroke and kill the ball in the right front corner. This may mean

Against such an opponent as Keeley, Strandemo is hard pressed to retain center court.

"fly-killing" the ball—taking it out of the air. In this shot be sure your wrist *does not break prior to contact*. If you "hear footsteps" and feel your foe is racing in to cover this shot, instantly change your plan and drive the ball past him, cross-court left.

If your opponent opts to drive the ball down the left wall, again you must cover the lane—which is a swatch about three feet wide down the left wall. Your advantage here is that most returns will be aimed at your backhand and you should be anticipating in that direction. Move into this lane and either kill the ball in the left corner with the same short, quick stroke, or drive it back across court to the right.

A bigger problem than regaining center-court position on serve returns is regaining it during a rally, especially a rally in which you find yourself on the move retrieving passing shots. It becomes essential that your defensive shots move your opponent out of the front court. You have two alternatives.

Try to hit a ceiling ball at the first opportunity. Even if you have to hit it down the forehand wall or, in some desperation, down the middle of the court, it will at least make your opponent move out of that precious center-court position, giving you time to regain it and set up again.

The alternative would be to hit the Z-ball. Again, the theory is to allow yourself enough time to regain the center court by making your opponent relinquish that precious piece of real estate. Working against you is the possibility that it will be more difficult to hit a Z-ball than a ceiling ball in this instance, but if you can manage it, the Z-ball here will be much more effective.

All other possibilities involve too much risk of a miscue. Don't even consider a kill attempt. Forget trying to pass when you're off balance and retrieving. And in this case the live ball works against you, because the lob is difficult to control.

## SUMMING UP STRANDEMO'S THEORY

Center-court position is one of the most important factors in your ascent to winning racquetball. No good player can win consistently without controlling the center court. As your racquetball game progresses, Strandemo says that "you should be drawn to center court as

Schmidtke momentarily claims center court and kills in the right-hand corner against Strandemo.

to a magnet. Your selection of shots should be geared to enable you to achieve that goal. Too many people are so impressed with top racquetball players skillfully scoring with kill shots that they forget—or don't realize—that many of these same kill shots were the result of good center-court positioning.''

It makes good racquetball sense that you will be more effective from center court at 20 feet from the front wall, no matter what shot you choose to take, than you will be from 39 feet in deep court. Football coach immortal Vince Lombardi used to say that football games are won in the ''pit,'' in the interior line. Center court is the ''pit'' of racquetball. It is where the games are won or lost.

To play winning racquetball, make center court your court of first resort!

# chapter seven

## RUBENSTEIN'S CHECKLIST

Another racquetball master and tournament winner, Ron Ruben-stein, has prepared a checklist for serious racquetball players. It doesn't vary too much from Charlie Brumfield's regimen, but it is more spare, more pragmatic, less theoretical—and perhaps the aspiring player can integrate what works best for him or her into a cohesive regimen.

1. Use the shaking-hands grip on your racquet, holding it as low as possible in the hand, with bottom finger off the racquet. The heel of the racquet should be in the middle of the palm.

2. Keep your eye on the ball, always.

3. Get your racquet way back before swinging.

4. Arm fully extended back.

# creative shooting

5. Wrist cocked.

6. Racquet about chest high.

7. As the ball comes—WAIT.

8. Remember at this point that shooting low rather than high moves the odds with you. If you come in with a good low shot, your opponent will have to race in to retrieve it, and then you'll have him way out of position. So THINK LOW!

9. Knees bent and ready.

10. Weight back, ready to shift. (As in golf and tennis.)

11. At contact with ball, weight moves forward and knees flex.

12. Arm straight.

13. Body faces side wall.

14. Back is bent.

Ron Rubenstein, left, was able to beat Steve Keeley in this match on the famous glass court at the Aurora, Illinois "Y" (where many of these pictures were taken).

15. Watch your footwork. Don't go off balance.

16. Develop a good follow-through. This will help you move fluidly into your next position.

17. After you've waited as long as possible before making contact with the ball, hit it about calf-high.

18. Racquet should be tilted up a little and cut through the ball, imparting a little downspin.

19. The wrist is firm as the ball is hit.

20. In the shifting of weight after the shot, pivot off the front foot and bring the weight around to carry the body toward the next shot.

Admittedly all of the above—in fact all instruction of this kind—sounds like a script for a slow-motion movie. And of course, that's pretty close to what we're doing. We're breaking down the motions and tactics of a complicated competitive game into individual components. There are great athletes with unorthodox styles, but the vast majority are stylistically orthodox. They've just learned to do the right things better.

# THE KILL

Rubenstein's special forte has been the backhand kill. The shot developed easily for him because he was a highly ranked tennis player before he moved to racquetball. "Tennis helped me get my racquet way back before swinging," he says. "In both tennis and racquetball you must get the racquet behind the ball and stride into it." (Charlie Brumfield holds that tennis players have to overcome many bad habits to play good racquetball.)

The purpose of any kill shot, of course, is to make a winning point. It also serves as a change of pace, and even if it misses slightly, it should upset your opponent. Developing a good backhand kill shot, Rubenstein feels, gives you twice as many chances at a good kill—and that many more chances at winning. If your game is off, of course, you have that much more opportunity to blow shots and lose.

It is important, therefore, that you develop confidence. The kill should be attempted when the player feels confident of making it. Confidence, of course, comes from practice. So—go thou forth and practice. . . .

One of the more important aspects of creative shooting lies in "reading" your opponent. Rubenstein feels that many players lose points by not analyzing their opponent's game and responses. As an example, he cites a simple, standard shot in an average racquetball game between two good club players: the ball off the back wall. Too many players try to put it away without regard to their opponent's position—and end up hitting it right back to their opponent—or duffing the shot.

To the pro, the ball off the back wall is a sure setup. He should be able to kill it or otherwise put it away seven out of ten times. The best shot to try off the back wall is the kill. Pros who feel they are in good position and know exactly where their opponent is will try this about 75 percent of the time, either backhand or forehand—and, of course, depending on their opponent's position. If an opponent is in front court, it's wiser to drive past him or go to the ceiling—but the advanced player must learn to take the shooting opportunities where he finds them, and the back wall is a good place to look. Racquetball is a very aggressive game and shooting is the most aggressive part of it.

The main kill shots to practice are: side wall-front wall; front wall-side wall; and straight front wall. The side wall-front wall kill can be hit from most places on the court but is most effective when you are near the backhand side wall and your opponent is somewhere near you. This shot can be varied by changing its speed and is the hardest of the three kills to retrieve—if the "kill" hasn't quite worked.

As your confidence in shooting grows, you should attempt to put a little backspin on the ball—kind of a chop as you hit it. If you do this properly, your side wall-front wall will die when it hits the front wall. This is a good shot to try when your opponent is behind you. The risk is that the ball will pop up for an easy return.

The front wall-side wall kill is used less frequently because its last angle is toward the middle of the court. A missed attempt here is a sure setup for your opponent. It would be wise for the up-and-coming player to practice hitting the side walls farthest away from him as a variation of this shot. The element of surprise works for you when, say, you hit the right side wall up front from a deep left-court position. You earn a winner and a glare from your opponent.

## MORE ON SPIN

Once you have developed into a good racquetball player and can feel the need and the urge and the drive to go on improving, you would do well to devote a few practice sessions to putting spin on the ball. All kinds of spin. All kinds of shots. All speeds. The object: observe how the impartation of English on a ball can alter its flight as you hit it. Without resorting to physics, the general area of curve balls, sliced balls, topped balls, and so on, is a difficult one to explain.

It is one of those things best observed in the doing. Even watching it being done by experts—one of the best possible ways to learn racquetball—leaves much to be learned by oneself. Watch the table tennis player, thirty feet back of the table, using an overhand slice to slow the ball, which then darts left or right as it hits the table. Curve pitchers, billiard players, and the great handball servers—Paul Haber, Kenny Schneider, Mort Leve—all are of the "English school."

Racquetball champion Steve Keeley believes that the ceiling ball's rise to popularity (by the introduction of Seamco's live ball a few years ago) has brought with it an inordinate amount of inaccuracy and imprecision. The advanced student, Keeley feels, should learn (1) proper spin; (2) the correct amount of power; and (3) the exact place on the ceiling he should hit for optimum effect.

Two out of three compliances with these laws just won't do. Next to hitting a small spot on the ceiling like a radar beam, the spin is hardest to acquire.

The player should practice bottom spin—the kind of spin with which most players naturally strike the ball anyway. It's something like slicing away at bologna in midair. Or trying to swat a fly on the lower half of the ball with your racquet. Try to swat the lower half of the fly while you're at it. This should give you the beginnings of a controllable bottom spin—when you learn to kill that fly again and again.

Bottom spin, in general, will cause the ball to bounce higher when it comes down, and will carry it farther after striking the floor than would a shot without spin. Undercutting, imparting bottom spin, killing that fly—whatever you call it—calls for many practice shots and almost defies explanation. It's one of those pragmatic situations, like learning to use a floor shift on a car. You've got to *feel* the way the clutch takes hold before you can drive smoothly. So practice until you get the *feel* of "spin."

When you've mastered the art of imparting bottom spin, stand in the rear of the court and try some overhand smashes with and without spin. Introduce spin—left spin and right spin—to your drives. Z-balls, cross-courts, even lobs, become additional shots for your arsenal with a touch of spin.

71

Keeley zips a shot past Rubenstein, its spin throwing Ron off.

72

When you've got a pretty good feel for spin, start using it on practice serves. As a fine young racquetball player with scant grammar has observed, "It's a whole nother ball game!"

# chapter eight

In no single department of sports is there more controversy than in the techniques of conditioning. Several hundred books earnestly attempt to solve the conditioning problem through diet. Vitamins and other panaceas have all had their turn at bat. Fortunately the human body is capable of shedding almost every abuse, shaking itself free, and rising to the task of going on with whatever activity its mind has programmed.

Without getting into one or another of the constantly warring camps on supplementary chemicals and foods that rush their strength-giving components right to your backhand or ankles, we would rather depend on what has become the conventional wisdom of conditioning and warming up.

No few lines in a book devoted to making you a winning racquetballer are going to force you away from the table before dessert is served. Or

# conditioning

will keep you off sweets, off excessive bread and sweet rolls, and away from sugar—that enemy disguised as an ally. If you don't have the determination to stop abusing your body—if that is indeed what you are doing—then all that can be offered you is one of the Greek principles that guided the early Olympians: Nothing in excess. (We speak of the *human* Olympians. The *mythic* Olympians wallowed in licentiousness and excess and became immortals anyway. Presumably, a remnant of this class still exists—big league baseball and football stars who drink, smoke, and party—and still retain their coordination.)

OK. Nothing in excess. And if you slide—why make an effort to halt the slide rather than continue downhill? Jean-Paul Sartre felt that Hell was other people. Maybe. But most of the would-be athletes we have known have been much tougher on themselves for slipping and

The physical demands made by racquetball at the pro level are considerable.

By the end of one game with equally hard-running Jerry Hilecher, and despite his excellent condition, Keeley looked like this.

backsliding from diet and exercise than anyone else could be. In this area, Hell is yourself. Preparing for a racquetball tournament, Steve Serot runs 15 miles a day. Through sand. Before his three hours of court practice.

Eighteen-year-old Marty Hogan likes to jog two miles a day. "The regularity of the running is important to me," says Hogan. "I feel awfully guilty if I miss a day." He also does calisthenics—in addition to his high school gym class regimen before he graduated—and then works out for two or three hours against the best competition he can find.

By all odds, jogging seems to be the most effective conditioner for racquetball players. The leg muscles, arm muscles, torso, and chest benefit from the circulatory demands made by jogging. And the wind gets better with consistency. So, if you can fill your mind with something to assuage the acknowledged boredom of the lonely runner, jogging is the closest activity we know to an all-around do-it-yourself conditioner.

But yet . . . If swimming is available to you, it is not very far behind. Probably the best-conditioned 43-year-old in the world, Chicago Lawson Y's Dick Woit, has swum a half mile a day for the past nine years. In addition to 1,000 push-ups, 300 sit-ups, an hour of leg lifts, lots of windsprints—and of course, some handball. Of course, conditioning is Woit's religion; he has "saved" many of Chicago's professional athletes after injuries.

The "experts" all seem agreed on the necessity for regularity, and on the wisdom of *gradually* accustoming the body to physical achievement beyond the simple demands of everyday life. So *after* your doctor assures you that you are well or fit enough to begin a regimen, try the walk-jog-walk-jog routine for half a mile a day, building up to a mile and then going on to wherever you feel comfortable—or to wherever your supply of spare time runs out.

No self-respecting instructional book would dare appear without recommending a "new" approach to some aspect of a sport. This book is no exception. We have recently come across two interesting publications. One bears the title *Flexibility Exercises,* and the subtitle "A Series of Flexibility Exercises Designed for Use in Physical Conditioning by Individuals, Athletic Teams and Physical Education Classes at All Age Levels." This heroic title covers the theories of Tennis Pro

An exciting new trend in conditioning, "Flexibility Exercises," developed by Scott and Nancy Cowgill of Louisiana, can be done in twosomes.

Scott Cowgill and his wife, Nancy Zingler Cowgill, an instructor in the Department of Physical Education at the University of S.W. Louisiana at Lafayette, Louisiana.

The second book, by Bob and Jean Anderson, of Englewood, Colorado, is called *Stretching*.

Both books extol the virtues of stretching the body in various ways, positions, and attitudes—in the interest of achieving flexibility and maximum utility from the old bag of muscle, bone, and fat.

The Cowgills (see pictures) advocate two types of stretching: ballistic and static. The ballistic type advocates a bouncing, snapping motion.

You extend the body's muscles and then move them in shorter bursts of extension. Static stretching involves stretching to a point and then holding that position. "When one reaches that point of stress," the Cowgills write, "a tingling sensation will occur in the stretched area, and this stretch should be maintained for approximately five seconds."

These exercises are repeated several times. The Cowgills have found that static stretching is less likely to cause injury during exercise and strongly advocate it. Starting from ground zero, it should take eight to twelve weeks of fifteen-to-twenty-minute-a-day stretchings to achieve the kind of flexibility that winning racquetball (or tennis or handball) requires.

If you are like most of us and don't like to run through regimens of any kind, one Cowgill tennis exercise is a real shorthand winner on the racquetball court. You hold the racquet behind your neck, top side up, and reach around with your other hand, behind your back, for the handle. Then you just keep tugging away in both directions—like a monomaniacal tug of war between left hand and right to get possession of the racquet. Two or three minutes of this before a game will really loosen the old arm muscles!

The Andersons include a similar exercise, but without the racquet. You just keep trying to reach over your own shoulder, down the back.

The Andersons have quantified their exercises for many sports, and their racquetball-handball warm-up stretches are exhaustive—if not exhausting, judging from Ms. Anderson's fine diagrams. The Andersons advocate that you:

1. Lie on your back with legs up for one to three minutes.
2. Reach over your shoulder with each arm for 30 seconds.
3. Swing your arms behind you for 15 seconds, one arm at a time.
4. Swing both arms behind you for 30 seconds.
5. Stretch your arms against a wall with hip parallel to wall.
6. Holding wall, bend from waist and hold for 30 seconds.
7. Sitting, touch toes for 30 seconds.
8. Sitting, pull legs into crotch for 30 seconds.
9. Repeat 7 and 8 for double the time.
10. From sitting position, twist body for 15 seconds while crossing one leg over other thigh.

Flexing the body readies it for action.

In another new system, "Stretching," Bob and Jean Anderson of Colorado advocate a series of warm-up stretches.

11. Repeat, other side.
12. Cradle leg in arms, lifting it, 30 seconds
13. Lying down on side, grab toes for 5 seconds.
14. Really pull at toes and elevate, 15 seconds.
15. Sitting up, curl leg behind you, 50 seconds.
16. Sitting up, extend one leg, curl the other, stretch for ankle with hands. 60 seconds.
17. (Repeat 12, 13, 14, 15, 16 for opposite leg.)
18. On back, knees up, hands behind neck, pull head up. 15 seconds.

19. Flat on back, arms on chest, one leg with knee crooked but sole on floor.

20. On back, hands behind head, roll hips, planting each leg on opposite side, across opposing knee. 20 seconds each side.

21. Lie on back, pull right thigh with left hand. 30 seconds a side.

22. 19 again.

23. On back, pull left knee back with hands. 20 seconds a leg.

24. Pull both legs back for 10 seconds.

25. Pull knees to forehead, making ball of yourself. 10 seconds.

26. On back, hands under hips, get legs over head until toes touch floor behind you. 45 seconds.

27. Roll out of this position slowly, holding ankles with hands, releasing "one vertebra" at a time. 40 seconds.

This is a 25-minute regimen, and depending on your condition, should leave you dog-tired and ready for bed—or full of ginger, ready for two hours of racquetball.

The Cowgill book starts with basic toe-touching and bent-trunk exercises, and progresses to stretching of the hamstrings and then real gymnastic straddles. One of their most useful contributions, we feel, is their series of exercises for two people at once. Basically, this involves sitting toe-to-toe with your partner, grasping arms, then "rowing" back and forth. Male-female couples can easily adapt some of the Cowgill exercises for conditioning togetherness and warming-up before mixed matches.

The Cowgills have also made a science of the old child's sport of rope-skipping, claiming that rope-skipping enhances agility, coordination, balance, rhythm, endurance, stamina, and aids in weight reduction. From single bounce to shuffle to straddle to heel-cross and grapevine, the Cowgills advocate rope-skipping as a natural variant of jogging and swimming.

# WARMING UP

The seemingly weird contortions made by professional athletes prior to running, pole vaulting, swimming, and everything else—including

The Cowgills demonstrate their flexibility.

Rope jumping is one of the best all-around conditioners and warm-ups.

the mutual pounding done by football players—have one basic concern: accustoming the body, gradually, to a forthcoming heroic demand. All of the conditioning done by serious athletes doesn't do much good unless they take those few minutes to get ready.

Most racquetball pros warm up on their game court or a nearby court with a series of jogs or fast walks around the court, in large circles.

85

A Cowgill exercise for tennists makes a fine stretcher for racquetballers, too, before matches.

Ron Rubenstein grins at the difference ten years makes in this exercise.

Most use some form of stretching—sit-ups, kneebends, touching the toes, bending sideways from the waist, stretching the arms.

Charlie Brumfield recommends that you start from the neck down. Rotate your neck until it feels loose. Rotate your shoulders. Twist and bend your trunk. Raise yourself on your toes. "Take your time when you warm up," he advises. "It's probably the most important part of your play, as far as prevention of injury is concerned."

For a tournament match, practice all of your shots when warming

87

Hundreds of repetitions of troublesome shots may be necessary before you master them. No one promises you a rose garden.

up. Forehand kills, forehand passes, forehand ceiling balls, forehand around-the-wall balls, volleys out of the air. Same shots with your backhand. Add back-wall shots, side-wall shots close to the walls, pinch shots, overheads.

If you warm up on a side court and are to play your tournament match under different or better lighting, get used to it. It's a different scene and adds a different dimension to the way the ball comes at you. Some pros like to look up right into the lights for a while until they get used to them. Then accustom yourself to the walls, especially if some are glass.

Most pros practice three to five hours a day—sometimes hitting a single shot 1,000 times until they get it right.

# chapter nine

By now you should be into a regular conditioning-and-practicing regimen, and trying to meet and beat players "better" than you. One of the best places to pick up the "feel" of winning racquetball is at a state or national tournament. To help you catch some of the excitement, we attended a national tournament at Burlington, Vermont, with camera and tape recorder.

It turned out to be an historic event. Seventeen-year-old Marty Hogan of St. Louis, one of racquetball's bright young stars, beat perennial champion Charlie Brumfield in the quarterfinals and went on to beat Steve Serot in the semis and Steve Keeley in the finals.

After his defeat, the 27-year-old Brumfield went back to the West Coast and practiced five hours a day, regaining his form—and winning the next two tournaments he entered.

# talking to the pros

We would like to share several informative interviews with you. One with two-time National Champion Bill Schmidtke—at 34, an "older" pro. We interviewed a top Maine amateur, Bill Doubord, right after Schmidtke defeated him. We interviewed college pro Dave Bledsoe, the "Southern Flash." We spoke with Jerry Hilecher, who has moved into the list of top ten racquetball players in the country. Charlie Drake, a Ph.D. in psychology, speaks on tactical racquetball. Then we interviewed young Richard Wagner, the only pro better looking than Robert Redford—and with nearly as many groupies. Wagner spoke at length about "anticipation."

## BILL SCHMIDTKE

**Q.** Bill, at 34 you've been a national champion several times and have

Most pros agree with Bill Schmidtke, who recommends watching as many players as you can who are better than you.

seen countless matches in addition to the ones you've played. What's the difference between the average player's game and the kind of play that moves a good player onward and upward? What does he or she have to do to improve?

**A.** There's no one answer, obviously, but the word "concentration" is high in the running for a description of the difference between fair, average racquetball—and good tournament play. Most beginners—and many "B" and "A" level club players—are so intent on returning the ball, they return it just anywhere, or nearly anywhere. They don't focus on a small area—read "concentrate" for focus. Learning exactly where the optimum area of return should be is a big part of self-improvement. It's the equivalent of the pro golfer narrowing his approach shots to a specific part of the green. The casual player is happy as hell just hitting the green. The pro wants a certain piece of that green. Similarly in racquetball. You've got to concentrate on the *where* of your return shot. Moving right along on the theme of concentration, the player determined to rise in class must learn to concentrate on *every shot* as if it were the 21st point of the game with the score tied at 20-20. After all, an early point tallies exactly the same as a late one, and because of your opponent's lack of concentration, may be easier to score.

**Q.** I just watched you win your quarterfinal match. Several times you seemed to be angry with yourself. How should the aspiring player deal with this common emotion? I mean, we've all seen people so angry at blowing a point, they proceed to blow the next four in a row.

**A.** Right! You saw me miss some setups—shots I should have put away easily. Sometimes your head miscalculates and signals that the shot is easier than it is. You lose concentration for a split second and *bingo!*—you've missed it. I keep coming back to concentration as the best lesson I can pass on to people who want to go deeper into this sport than using it as a weekend social thing. Concentration and focus.

**Q.** When you play a lesser player, what happens to your game?

**A.** Unfortunately you sometimes get a little lazy. So the lesser player tastes a little blood and begins to concentrate on killing you— which he sometimes does. Once you lose the momentum, you've nearly lost the game. If you let up for even a short time, a good average player can score lots of points on, say, a better above-average player. That's why so many racquetball matches—and tennis matches for that matter—go into more games than they should.

**Q.** What about conditioning? At 34, you like to joke that your legs are twice as old as Marty Hogan's.

**A.** True, true. Aging in athletes occurs mostly in the legs. I'm the oldest pro on the tour except for Rubenstein. I've been playing the longest—and on days like this, after two matches, you feel it. Jogging is the obvious conditioner for legs, but I don't get the kick out of it that most racquetball players do. I think that aging in this sport comes 90 percent in the legs. It's been that

Against Bill Doubord, Schmidtke's forehand worked well.

Legs that have lived twice as long as Marty Hogan's take more conditioning and more warming up before a match.

way for me. After I won the Nationals in 1974, I kind of relaxed and didn't do much running. I guess I could have used some. Just a few years before, in 1971, I beat Craig Finger. Of course, in 1974, I beat Steve Serot, who was then 18 and a strong runner out on those California beaches. You know, about legs—it's not that they hurt especially. It's just that they slow down a fraction of an inch at a time and they don't take you *exactly* where you want to be *exactly* when you want to be there. I'm talking of *precision*—another good word for the aspiring racquetball player. Your head is there, but your knees aren't. So it's never too late, folks. For the past four weeks—and continuing now permanently as long as I play seriously, I'll be running a mile up a hill every day. If I feel up to it, I'll run down, too. It'll take a couple of months to feel the results, but just in this tournament I feel results already. I've caught myself over-running the ball! That hadn't happened in a long time. It shakes up the old computer, but there it is. Good conditioning—no matter how you do it—and achievement in this sport, as in every other sport, go hand in hand. Come to think of it, until these matches I hadn't over-run the ball for a year or so.

**Q.** In general, how do good young players stack up against good older players? What I'm getting at is how a good younger player can improve himself or herself.

**A.** It's amazing how well young players of both sexes can hit the ball these days. It's like pre-season baseball, where the kids keep hitting them out of the park and all look like Joe DiMaggio or Willie Mays—until they hit big-league pitching in earnest. Well, perhaps the mental factor is equally important. Without going into way-out sports psychology—which is kind of fashionable these days—I think younger players basically have a head problem. They're not thinking ahead and planning ahead on the court—or if they are, they are not doing it as effectively as the older player. The young player tends to be a great retriever, and the older player pushes him or her into a kind of defensive game—with a few sparks emerging with successful kill shots. I think all of the top players in the sport are close to equal at shooting the ball exactly where they want it. But those words ''close to'' leave a lot of room. Some of that room is in execution. No one is a machine about executing shots. But the trick is to develop your execution of your shots to a degree of machine-like consistency. If you can do this, you can run your opponent all over the place and keep your offensive going. So it comes down to practicing for consistency and accuracy, hour after hour.

**Q.** What's your favorite shot?

**A.** The forehand kill shot. I think I do it with great accuracy.

**Q.** I noticed that you were hitting four out of six corner kills within a foot of the corner—where I happened to be sitting. Is this usual for you?

**A.** On a good day. Mostly, however, when you start to hit with accuracy in practice or early in a match, you try to forget about

96

Schmidtke's forehand kill against Bledsoe.

that particular shot and hope that the shot becomes automatic—just a part of your arsenal without thinking about it. If you start thinking about shots, you add a couple of mental microseconds that sometimes cause you to miss. Microseconds—that's what this game is all about. The way Birdie Tebbetts said that baseball was a game of inches. A fraction of an inch's change on where the ball and bat meet could mean the difference between a pop fly and a home run that wins the pennant or the Series.

**Q.** So what does it come down to? What's the bottom line for the person who wants to play winning racquetball?

**A.** In a few words, consistency and accuracy. You get accuracy by practicing to become consistent. Hit the same kind of shot the same way in practice. Use the same kind of approach and power wherever possible. Work these shots and this consistency into your game the way you would build your body—step by step, day by day. For example, I'm always practicing my backhand because I know it needs improvement. It's still a better defensive shot for me than offensive. I suppose it's important to know your limitations, too. As you get older it's a good idea to develop an accurate soft shot. I find my soft shots save me a lot of energy. Somehow young players generally bypass this important shot. I'd advise young people to work on a good change-of-pace soft shot. If you noticed my last match, I beat my young opponent with soft shots. I caught him hanging back, so I dumped it in the corner. The main thing is to use what you have. If you're young, use your legs and power. If you're older, use whatever the heck you can. The ambitious player starts thinking like this: He can tell where he's goofing up, or better, where in the sequence he needs work. It's important for the winning racquetball player to progress without having his bad habits harden. Progress continues as long as you can build. When you become set in patterned responses and can't break out of them, you may only be 24 years old, but it's too late to help you very much. The name of the game, of course, is to develop good habits, and to use these tools in the execution of good tactics.

Soft shots, such as this lob, save energy for older players.

# BILL DOUBORD

**Q.** Bill, you have just lost to former National Champion Bill Schmidt-ke. He's considerably older than you, somewhat slower, but of course, much more experienced. What did you learn while losing to Schmidtke?

**A.** Well, I should explain that my current level of play is among the top four amateur players in Maine. I generally win or place high in the regional amateur tournaments around home. The things I learned here kind of knock me out. You say he's somewhat slower than I. Well, on the court I got the impression he was twice as fast as I. And what's more, knew exactly where I was going to hit the ball—even before I did. He would retrieve, and before I could get over my surprise at his retrieving what would easily go for a kill shot at home, he would kill it against me. Or as some joker in the stands said, "He re-kills all your killers." It takes a real winner to score a point on a pro like Schmidtke. Each time I would—not often enough, of course—I would become more aware of his class—like a couple of steps up ahead of me. Giving me something to work for, of course. Man, I can't wait to get home and practice cross-court kill shots. Obviously I should have tried to shoot away from Bill more, get the ball out of his reach. . . .

**Q.** Make believe a good local player came to you and asked how he could improve his game. How should he work towards beating you? What would you tell him?

**A.** Practice, man. And conditioning. I'm only 28, but Schmidtke ran me ragged. Also, I'd advise a younger player to drive for everything. If I see a shot and figure I can't get to it—or it'll be close—I generally quit on it, to conserve energy. The pros— they just keep going and trying—and making those shots. I would tell the local player to devote all the time he could to shot-making, conditioning and, as Bill says, developing consistency.

# DAVE BLEDSOE

**Q.** Dave, as one of the rising stars of racquetball, and incidentally

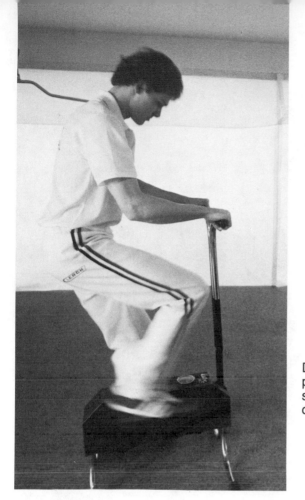

Dave Bledsoe
prefers jogging but
sometimes uses gym
devices.

the best dancer of the racquetball pros, what message do you
have for players who want to improve their game?

**A.** You have to work hard on each department of the game, all the
individual shots, from serving to defensive ceiling shots. And I
mean work for hours at a time. That's one advantage young
players have: They usually have more time on their hands, so
they should use it to develop. Once you've built up a repertoire
of shots, then you start concentrating on game-plan strategy and
working your best possible game against your opponent. Most
of all, you have to be confident in all departments. Mike Zeitman and I beat Charlie Drake and Marty Hogan playing doubles
a few months ago. No matter how great Hogan is at singles, you

Bledsoe gets a little more competition than he can handle from Brumfield.

could tell he wasn't into doubles playing—not that I'm that great, of course. But you could tell, if he really got interested, just how much work even he would need to play good doubles. I like that left wall and did pretty well killing and passing down that side. Of course Zeitman was *on* that day. Now there's a player who's hot and cold. I don't know how to advise someone like that, except to practice the shots you seem coldest on. To sum it up, your ambitious player must be a worker—or forget it. You can't pick a title off a page—but you can get somewhere reading a roadmap. You can get there if you go out and drive, drive, drive.

Bledsoe's quickness surprises Sohmidtke.

**Q.** Right. What about competition?

**A.** Competition is vital to improvement. My trouble is that these kids improve faster than I ever can, being younger. Teaching young people not to choke up is something we try in San Diego. We set up game situations, something like football coaches do. "You're behind 20-15. You're serving against Brumfield . . ." And so on.

**Q.** It seems that most of the champions have been hitting the top in their late twenties and early thirties. Is this changing now, with players like Serot, Wagner, and Hogan?

**A.** Well, we've had champions in their late thirties. Paul Haber was national handball champ from the time he was 30 to 34 approximately. It seems as if there is a certain maturity factor in the court sports—look at the ancient guys who dominate squash. But of course, tennis has seen the age come down, and that's what racquetball is doing right now. The sport hasn't been growing as fast as tennis—but in proportion, maybe more so, with all the new court clubs going up. Tennis's junior camps are spewing out top-rate players by the dozens. I think that's about to happen in racquetball. Leach, I feel, is doing its part in this trend. We're introducing four-day clinics that will travel across the U.S., bringing six top players to local clubs to encourage and train good players—of all ages and both sexes. You know, incidentally, racquetball is one sport where women's liberation arrived early. The game is absolutely the same for both sexes. Last year's three-wall open in Toledo had Kathy Williams beat Sue Carow in the women's singles—and a couple of hours later show up as Dan Alder's partner in open doubles. Both Jack Soble and Jerry Davis—who lost the first game 20-21 before winning the next two—agreed that Kathy Williams was one of the toughest competitors they had ever faced.

## JERRY HILECHER

**Q.** Jerry, you're one of the fastest young players—well, not as young as Hogan or Serot, but still in your early twenties. Tell us about yourself.

**A.** I began playing seriously at the University of Missouri about four years ago. I won the first intercollegiate tournament, at the

(Facing page.) Women make up more than a third of racquetball's growing army. In this picture by one of my students, Gail Rietze (covering her first racquetball match!), little Sue Carow and Kathy Williams collide in a tournament final won by Williams.

Jerry Hilecher
practices three hours
a day.

University of Illinois at Champaign, Illinois. I then won the
national doubles in Canada playing with Bill Schmidtke. So I'm
still working hard.

**Q.** How would you advise good players on how to improve their
game?

**A.** The obvious answers are work, competition, exercise—but I
presume everyone says that in one way or another. The thing is,
no matter how many times these things are said, students of the
game are always looking for shortcuts. My experience has been
that most players can only play so much racquetball before they
reach a kind of plateau and level off. At that point my advice is
for them to go to some tournaments as observer or player. This
along with a regular conditioning program, of course. The body
is still the fortress from which we all do battle. At tournaments

106

Hilecher aims at higher plateaus.

you find out what your weaknesses are—so you make up your mind to go out and work on those weaknesses. You know, in some tournaments I don't care if I won or not. I'm there to practice just one or two things I think will improve my game in the long run. Winning isn't enough—no matter what the great football coach Vince Lombardi said. You've got to build your game so victory will be a natural result, not a one-or-two-time thing.

**Q.** What about mental attitude?

**A.** Well, everybody's got a different style, but the main difference between the advanced player and the pro is concentration. I've taught myself to get psyched up and be alert. I kind of yell at myself, scold myself, push myself, talk to myself, encourage myself, and try to block out any fatigue I feel, knowing I can rest afterwards. I direct all this psyching at myself, not my op-

107

"At tournaments you find out what your weaknesses are."

Another flier in the tradition of Keeley and Serot, Hilecher is moving up fast.

ponent. I know other players rely on staying calm and quiet. But I like to drive myself. Steve Serot used to yell and scream at himself, and then for a year or so he stopped. Then I noticed, in the New England finals against Hogan, after he injured himself, he came back actually roaring at himself—and despite his injury to his shooting elbow—he almost captured the match. The crowd loved seeing this quiet guy suddenly roar. Of course, then you have Charlie Brumfield, who's a master at psyching out his opponent—but that's a different story. I'm talking about getting yourself up. You can just feel Steve Strandemo concentrating. That's how he gets such a good jump on the ball. Steve Keeley stays fairly quiet, but sometimes he yells at himself.

**Q.** Do you get angry at yourself?

**A.** For sure. And it hurts my game sometimes. If I really feel bad, I'll call time out and calm down. You've got to learn to control yourself just the way you have to learn to control the ball. Sure, like anyone else, I get mad at the referee if I think he called a bad shot or if my opponent skips a ball in and gets away with it. My main advice to aspiring players is attend tournaments, work on your weaknesses, and try to keep your anger under control. It's something like judo. You can make a missed shot work toward the next shot—rather than against it. Just add that miss to your mental attitude, and make it help you focus and concentrate on the immediate future. Drive the immediate past from your mind. There are no points in it.

## CHARLIE DRAKE

**Q.** Charlie, you're known as a fantastic competitor and also as an official of the Leach Company, which is doing so much for racquetball. Tell us about yourself.

**A.** There's nothing much to tell, Art. I've been the Canadian National Doubles champion—with a great partner, of course. I've been California Singles champ a couple of times. I've been on the pro tour three years, and I've come close to winning—but haven't so far.

**Q.** You are known for your work with the younger players—Serot, Keeley, Wagner, and so on. How do you work with them— keeping in mind this book is for fairly good players who want to become winners?

**A.** That's the name of the game—winning. We train a lot of local kids around San Diego. The boys are referred to as "The Leach Stable." We're sort of the national Mecca for young racquetball players—even the St. Louis kids come out there! We work hard on a player's attitudes and encourage him—or her—to play two to four hours a day. We practice on mental errors— mind-wandering mistakes and lapses. We also try to develop

Leach executive pro Charlie Drake serves as godfather to the young pros, who beat him regularly.

positive mental attitudes—towards winning, for example, and of course, towards conditioning. We work hard on serving and return of serves. We work on making the right shot at the right time, and bear down hard on the court strategies that are necessary when you're winning, losing, when you have the momentum, when you want the momentum.

**Q.** What about conditioning?

111

**A.** It's so obvious that conditioning is a big part of the game, it's easy to assume every would-be player knows that he or she has to run, swim, bike ride or something for a couple of hours a day. In addition to court practice, of course. I'm talking about serious players—which is the subject, right?

**Q.** How can the amateur who can't wait for the tour to hit his home area improve his or her game?

**A.** The important thing for this person is to find a partner of equal or superior skills. You've got to have someone capable of pushing you and punishing you for your mistakes on the court. Just getting out there with a hacker isn't going to improve you. It might even have the opposite effect. And he or she should start entering tournaments as soon as possible. That's where a player learns if he has it to go on towards better play than he's doing.

**Q.** Do good players rise to the top? Are there any great undiscovered phenoms around? Like undiscovered Muhammad Alis who could polish him off if only they got the match?

**A.** I doubt it. Look at this tournament (New England Pro-Am 1975). It was open to everybody. But right now the 16 players left in the tournament are all pros. There isn't any outsider. To repeat, the aspiring player must find good competition, and rank himself or herself, gradually hoping by practice and will power to move upward.

**Q.** When you train, what's your favorite method?

**A.** When I'm training for a match, aside from the obvious jogging and sit-ups, I work in solitary sessions of 1,000 shots. This usually takes about an hour and a half. Then I look around for some serious youthful competition like Steve Serot or Richard Wagner—and am lucky to get off the court alive.

# RICHARD WAGNER

**Q.** Richard, as one of the new, young breed of professional rac-

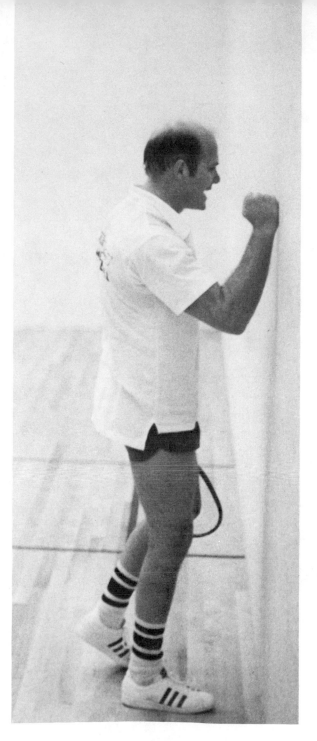

It is bottor to dircot
your anger at a
wall than to let it
work its way
through your own
body and mind,
the shrinks tell us.

Anticipation is Rich Wagner's middle name.

114

quetball players, you have played some fantastic games—winning some and losing others against the very greatest names in the sport. Here at New England, in beating John Spencer, you looked as if no one in the world could beat you. When I mentioned that observation to Drake, he said, "Yes. If he had gone on to play like that, no one in the world could have beaten him." Unfortunately you just didn't go on like that.

**A.** I know, I know. But the thing to do is pick yourself up and work, work, work.

**Q.** There is no doubt in anyone's mind that you will be in the very top handful of racquetball players within the next three years. Your blazing speed and court savvy—when you're hot—are incomparable, and things of beauty and grace to observe. In this book we're trying to help the good, average player move upward and play winning racquetball rather than merely competitive racquetball. How can a slow player seemingly cover the court better and quicker than a fast player? Why does one player seem to be able to pick up many more shots in the front court, while another, equally speedy opponent, cannot?

**A.** The answer lies in a single word: anticipation. Anticipation is the combination of speed and quickness, often thought of as the same things, but actually far different. You can't time anticipation like you can speed, for anticipation is as much mental as it is physical.

The importance of anticipation in racquetball is immense. No top player can survive without good anticipation, and all of the outstanding competitors also have outstanding anticipation. Often anticipation can overcome the actual lack of speed to improve a player's game.

This is true of current National Champion Charlie Brumfield, probably the slowest player in the top ten today. But Charlie is unequaled in his ability to cover the court, to anticipate his opponent's shots and thereby increase his chances of winning.

Anticipation is important for a variety of reasons, any one of which should be enough to cause the learning racquetball player to perk his or her ears. The most obvious and general improvement in one's game due to anticipation is better court coverage.

That extra step or step-and-a-half due to increased anticipation means picking up kill attempts and re-killing them rather than having them be double-bounce pick-ups and points for your opponent. It means the ability to cut off passes rather than having to scurry frantically into back court on retrieving efforts. And it also means being able to reach and set up for countless shots that otherwise would have been uncoordinated lunges.

Greater anticipation has many other benefits. For one, it allows the player a greater margin of error on his or her shots. For example, if you can cover the front court well, your kills need not be quite as low as would be the case if you were not a good front court coverer. Even if your opponent can pick up your kill attempt, he will be forced to rush his return and you will be right there to put it away.

Conversely, a player with good anticipation puts the pressure on his opponent to make a sure winner of his shots, thus increasing the margin of error still more. If your opponent knows you can get almost everything in front court he also knows his kills must be virtual roll-outs; and this pressure often will cause him to skip more shots than usual, or in some cases abandon entirely his kill attempts in favor of passes.

A final advantage to the player with good anticipation is that it delays the often fast-rushing fatigue factor. By being able to reach balls with that extra step, you might be saving five, six, or even ten steps on that one shot alone. By being able to set up for shots, you eliminate the franticness of retrieving, also a factor in fatigue.

All in all, increasing your anticipation will increase your skill and your number of racquetball victories. So, how do you increase this nebulous factor of the game?

The first thing the player must do is get into condition. A well-conditioned racquetballer is well on his way to being a quicker and better anticipatory athlete. If your body is tired, your mind, no matter how great the desire, cannot instill life into those

Anticipating a lob in front of Bledsoe.

throbbing legs. There are a variety of conditioning programs both on and off the court, including running and playing. Many of these programs have been presented in *National Racquetball Magazine*. They make up a list of mandatory reading and then mandatory doing. The first step toward increased anticipation is getting into shape.

As for specific, on-the-court tricks to aid anticipation, there are many. The first and most obvious is to watch the ball at all times. There is no way a player can get a good jump on any shot if he doesn't know where the shot is, from where it was hit, or where it is going. Many beginning players are guilty of not watching the ball, especially after the serve. As server, you must turn and see where your serve went and what kind of return your opponent hits. After all, if your opponent shoots the ball, you'll have to move in; if the return is a ceiling ball, you'll have to move back. If you don't watch the ball, how can you possibly know which way to move until it's too late?

Watching the ball is important on every single shot of a rally, not just the serve. It is the basic fundamental of racquetball, and the key to anticipation.

Anticipation can be increased if the player takes a little time to analyze his game and his shots. Do my ceiling balls carry into deep court? If they do you can anticipate a ceiling return. Do my ceiling balls come up short, or off the back wall? If so, expect an offensive return.

The same analyzation holds true for every shot you hit. You have chosen a particular shot either to end the rally or to extend it. Each shot has a specific goal, the reason you hit it. That goal is to force a certain return by your opponent. By being able to accomplish this, you have not only gained control of the rally, you have increased the percentages of anticipation on your behalf.

As an example of this, let's take the serve. Good serves are vital to any player's success, and those players with effective serves can anticipate their opponents' returns easily. If I serve a garbage serve to your backhand, and the ball reaches you at chest or shoulder height, I immediately recognize many factors.

Two of the quickest players alive, Serot and Wagner, are caught in a shared instant of concentration and anticipation.

First, you will not shoot that serve. The ball is too high to go for bottom board, and too low for any kind of reverse overhead. If you want to go for the kill on this shot, I'll give it to you every time, and I'll also beat you, badly.

I doubt seriously that you'll attempt a pass off this serve, either. As a surprise maneuver, maybe, but a down-the-line or cross-court pass is very difficult to control on a garbage serve. And remember, I'm standing in center court. No, you won't pass.

You will hit a ceiling ball. It's really your only possible effective shot off a well-hit garbage serve. And I know it, meaning I will be anticipating a ceiling return, and reach it effortlessly.

What if I hit a poor serve? Well, let's say I hit a low, hard drive again to your backhand and it comes off the back wall near the left wall. Now I'm in trouble, yet by anticipation I will increase my chances of reaching your shot.

I know you'll hit an offensive return, so I can eliminate all thought of your going to the ceiling, as long as you have had time to set up. If you go for the kill, you will most likely shoot it to the left corner, it being a far easier shot than trying a backhand hypotenuse kill off the serve. So now I have eliminated the back one-third of the court, and the front right corner. If you roll off the serve to that left corner, I won't be able to pick it up anyhow, so my coverage need not worry about the true winner, only the shot that is left up.

If you attempt a pass, you've made it a little tougher on me. My serve was poor enough to give you a good choice of down-the-line or cross-court. In general, most players stand around the center of the service zone when they serve, and their first step is generally toward the left wall, anticipating a return to their backhand (right-handed players). Also, since I'm still wary of you shooting into the left corner, I would be leaning left. This means I will reach your down-the-line pass.

If any of the above makes sense to you, good—only a flat roll-out in the left corner, or a cross-court pass to the right will beat me, even though I have hit a poor serve. And these are the two hardest shots to hit with accuracy in racquetball. Anything else

Springing from anticipation into action takes reflexes like these.

A classic view of one great player watching another's every move.
Rich Wagner focuses on Marty Hogan.

you hit, or if you are not extremely accurate with either of those
two shots, I will not only return, but be in good position to put
you out.

A lot can be learned by watching your opponent. Many times a
player will telegraph his upcoming shot, like a basketball player
telegraphs his pass or a pitcher telegraphs fast ball or curve.

Does he dip his shoulder when going for a kill? How soon
does he commit himself? Does he bring his racquet as far back
for a pass as he does for a ceiling return? How far does he let the
ball drop? Can he hit overheads?

A lot of the above can be learned by studying your opponent. If he is a daily or weekly adversary, you can learn a great deal. Does he tend to shoot serves? Does he like to "go for it" when a shot comes off the back wall? How is his backhand? Can he go to the ceiling a couple of times, or does he prefer to drive the ball? Is his forehand deadly? What are his favorite serves? Does he ever rush the serve? All of these are questions you should ask yourself about your opponent. If you take the time to study and analyze not only your own game, but his too, you will be far better off.

Experience is another factor in improving your anticipation. Experience in the sense of knowing the walls. Top pro Bill Schmidtke is great at this. As his opponent hits virtually any shot, Bill has the uncanny ability to instantaneously figure out where that shot will end up. He never takes an unnecessary step. Where the average player might take three steps right to try and retrieve a pass, the top player like Bill would take three steps sure enough, but back and diagonally right. Same exertion, but one player reaches the shot and the other does not.

In the above situation, the faster player might not get the ball, but Schmidtke, not known for his speed, will get it. Simply by knowing the walls.

Anticipation is not just guessing where your opponent will hit the ball. It is far more. It is something that can be practiced and improved. Anticipation can take the good player and make him great. Lack of it can make the potentially great player a frustrated also-ran. But anybody can improve his anticipation. Try it, and see if your game doesn't improve along the way.

# chapter ten

Racquetball's official rules, like the regulations in most sports, leave a significant amount of latitude when explaining what a player can or cannot do. A smart player can use the rules to his or her advantage; in fact, all top players know the rules explicitly and do exactly that. The official rules of the U.S. Racquetball Association, supplied free of charge to members of that organization, are considered mandatory equipment for any player desiring to establish a winning racquetball game.

The most common rule that is used by players to aid their game is the "ten-second rule." This regulation allows either the server or receiver ten seconds to serve (server) or be ready to receive (receiver).

Often, inexperienced players will win a rally, gather in the ball, step right up, and serve again. Such a procedure does not use the ten-second rule to its full advantage.

# a primer
# on using the rules
# by chuck leve*

The professional player will use a large portion of the ten seconds before serving. His head is clear, he mentally surveys what serves have been effective, and which serve he feels will lead to the weakest return. The smart player will concentrate on his serve. Remember, only when serving can one player actually stand and take a free shot, to put the ball in as difficult a position as possible. The good player will use the advantage, coupled with the ten-second rule, to make his serve the best possible.

Another method of using the ten-second rule to your advantage is to combat fatigue. If you are tired or tiring, use the full nine or ten seconds before serving or being ready to receive. If you are the receiver,

*the chief referee at most pro tournaments.

125

The loneliest and sometimes bravest man at a match is the referee. Here Chuck Leve, silhouetted on the Aurora balcony, watches Bledsoe and Brumfield in a final.

don't let the server rush you into the next rally. Pull up your socks, adjust your grip, wipe your glasses, adjust your headband, and if all else fails, turn your back to the server. Just be sure you're ready to receive within the allotted ten seconds. In tournament play, if you're not ready and the server serves, you are obligated to return it.

The rule that allows two serves to get the ball in play is another regulation that many good players use to their advantage. Since you get another try in the event of a long, short, or three-wall serve, many players go for an ace in their first serve. A low, hard drive aimed just behind the short line is the most common attempt at the ace. If the ball is short, then the server will use a softer, safer serve on his second try. Beginning and intermediate players should use this first serve as a

Player's-eye view of the referee.

means of practicing their hard serves. There is nothing to lose.

If you are tired, or looking to gain a psychological edge on your opponent, some players will serve long or short purposely, to gain the time. By serving long, having the ball rebound all the way back to front court, and slowly walking to pick the ball up again, you will have gained almost 30 seconds of additional rest. This was a favorite ploy of Charlie Brumfield, national champion in 1972, 1973, and 1975, to gain much-needed rest.

There is a two-sided effect of using the long serve, the first being the above-mentioned rest. Secondly, and sometimes more effectively, the long serve frustrates your opponent. Often a player will initially use this ploy to gain rest, and once it proves effective, he will continue to utilize it. It can be a means of slowing or even stopping opponent

127

Keeley uses wipe-up timeout to rest, and Ron Rubenstein doesn't
mind a bit.

momentum. Once you manage to get your opponent thinking about the long serve rather than the serve return, you have succeeded in gaining the psychological edge. And in close matches, sometimes this is all you need to turn defeat into victory.

Another common use of the rules is not actually in the rule book; however, through interpretation it has become possibly the most common method of gaining additional rest. Simply, it is calling for a towel from the referee and wiping the floor when it becomes wet with perspiration. It is the referee's obligation to see that the playing surface is safe at all times, and when enough perspiration accumulates, the floor must be wiped. Since the referee is often far from the court floor, he must take the player's word for it that the floor is in fact wet.

In close matches many players dive for balls near or out of their reach, a maneuver that causes a wet floor virtually every time. Although diving is not recommended procedure as a means of getting the floor wet (too much of an injury risk), any time your body ends up on the floor, the floor will become wet. And since there is no rule in the books saying exactly how much time you have to wipe up the floor (referee's discretion) you should use as much as possible.

In more and more major tournaments, tournament officials are employing a person to stand outside the door of the court with a mop, and at the referee's direction, mop the floor quickly and fully. However, in big tournaments, with eight or ten courts being used at once, this is impossible.

Minor injuries are another area where the smart player will use the rules to his advantage. The rules allow an individual player 15 minutes in injury time-outs per match, per injury. The 15 minutes is figured cumulatively, meaning that if you take a five-minute injury time-out in game one, you still have ten minutes for that same injury later in the match, if it is necessary. No more than three time-outs are allowed for any single injury.

We are not advocating that a player fake an injury. This would be unsportsmanlike conduct and could result in forfeiture of the match. What we do advocate is that when a minor injury does occur, use the time given you under the rules, i.e., don't be a martyr. If you have jammed your ankle, walk it off, take some practice shots, relace your shoes, and do anything else necessary for you to feel comfortable.

Wagner's dying fawn may have been held several beats longer than necessary. Who can tell?

There is no rush. If you find yourself in this condition, make sure the referee keeps track of any injury minutes charged against you, if you need a time-out. Usually, if you just walk around a bit, and take just a few practice shots, you will not be charged with an injury time-out.

Any good player should be familiar with all the rules of racquetball, but the above are a few of the most important. Another is the rule of ball replacement in the event the ball breaks during play.

Although not nearly as common as in the early days of racquetball, there are still instances where the ball will break during play. When this occurs, the rally during which the ball broke is replayed. Usually there is no question regarding the implementation of the rule. However, there are occurrences when the ball will break and nobody will be able to tell. Once that ball is put into play again, i.e., is served, the

Five minutes' rest between first and second games. Ten minutes between second and third. Anything else you can scrounge depends on your ingenuity.

Strandemo likes to make tapes of other players and of himself. Some players feel that electronics will eventually be used to help referees make calls. Probably football replays will be the first usage.

previous rally stands no matter if the ball is broken or not.

Therefore, if for any reason you as player think the ball might be broken, it is imperative to request that the referee inspect the ball. Of course, you must do this prior to its being put in play again. This is your right under the rules, and unless you abuse it, could save you a key point from time to time.

Both players are allowed five minutes between the first and second games, and ten minutes' rest between the second and third games, if the third game is necessary. Smart players will utilize the time between games. The player who goes off to the locker room, downs a thirst-quencher, and sits around may find himself having a great deal of difficulty getting loose for game number three.

The intelligent player will use five or six minutes of the ten to catch his breath, but he will return to the court with at least three minutes left between games to begin loosening up. The beginning of the third game is like the beginning of the match, only it is a one-game match. If you are not ready to play full-force at the beginning of the third game, you could find yourself on the short end of a big score without breaking a sweat. Additionally, you could find yourself pulling a muscle or otherwise injuring yourself due to inadequate warm-up.

So take your five or six minutes of rest and then go back to the court and go through an abbreviated version of your normal pre-game warm-up. Do some stretching exercises, normal body looseners, and, of course, enough forehand, backhand, and overhead shots to fully loosen up all the muscles. Ideally, you should break a slight sweat just before the start of the third game.

Like the manager of a baseball team, a racquetball player should know everything there is in the rule book. Unlike the baseball player, the racquetballer does not have the manager to fall back on for this knowledge. The racquetball player has to be his own player and coach during a match.

There is nothing illegal about using the rules as described above to your advantage. All good players do it, and you will actually be at a disadvantage if you are not aware of all the rules and how to use them.

The rules are dry, but some of them can be cut closely. Players can
always appeal, but referees don't find them appealing.

# appendix

# official racquetball rules of the united states racquetball association (u.s.r.a.) and national racquetball club

## FOUR WALL RULES

### Part I. The Game

**Rule 1.1—Types of Games.** Racquetball may be played by two or four players. When played by two it is called "singles"; and when played by four, "doubles."

**Rule 1.2—Description.** Racquetball, as the name implies, is a competitive game in which a racquet is used to serve and return the ball.

**Rule 1.3—Objective.** The objective is to win each volley by serving or returning the ball so the opponent is unable to keep the ball in play. A serve or volley is won when a side is unable to return the ball before it touches the floor twice.

**Rule 1.4—Points and Outs.** Points are scored only by the serving side when it serves an ace or wins a volley. When the serving side loses a volley it loses the serve. Losing the serve is called a "hand-out."

**Rule 1.5—Game.** A game is won by the side first scoring 21 points.

**Rule 1.6—Match.** A match is won by the side first winning two games.

## Part II. Court and Equipment

**Rule 2.1—Court.** The specifications for the standard four-wall racquetball court are:

**(a) Dimension.** The dimensions shall be 20 feet wide, 20 feet high, and 40 feet long, with back wall at least 12 feet high.

**(b) Lines and Zones.** Racquetball courts shall be divided and marked on the floors with 1½-inch-wide red or white lines as follows:

**(1) Short Line.** The short line is midway between and is parallel with the front and back walls dividing the court into equal front and back courts.

**(2) Service Line.** The service line is parallel with and located 5 feet in front of the short line.

**(3) Service Zone.** The service zone is the space between the outer edges of the short and service lines.

**(4) Service Boxes.** A service box is located at each end of the service zone by lines 18 inches from and parallel with each side wall.

**(5) Receiving Lines.** Five feet back of the short line, vertical lines shall be marked on each side wall extending 3 inches from the floor. See rule 4.7(a).

**Rule 2.2—Ball Specifications.** The specifications for the standard racquetball are:

**(a) Official Ball.** The official ball of the U.S.R.A. is the black Seamco 558; the official ball of the N.R.C. is the green Seamco 559; or any other racquetball deemed official by the U.S.R.A. or N.R.C. from time to time. The ball shall be 2¼ inches in diameter; weight approximately 1.40 ounces with the bounce at 68-72 inches from 100-inch drop at a temperature of 76 degrees F.

**Rule 2.3—Ball Selection.** A new ball shall be selected by the referee for use in each match in all tournaments. During a game the referee may, at his discretion or at the request of both players or teams, select another ball. Balls that are not round or which bounce erratically shall not be used.

**Rule 2.4—Racquet.** The official racquet will have a maximum head length of 11 inches and a width of 9 inches. These measurements are computed from the outer edge of the racquet head rims. The handle may not exceed 7 inches in length. Total length and width of the racquet may not exceed a total of 27 inches.

**(a)** The racquet must include a thong which must be securely wrapped on the player's wrist.

**(b)** The racquet frame may be made of any material, as long as it conforms to the above specifications.

**(c)** The strings of the racquet may be gut, monofilament, nylon, or metal.

**Rule 2.5—Uniform.** All parts of the uniform, consisting of shirt, shorts and socks, shall be clean, white or of bright colors. Warm-up pants and shirts, if worn in actual match play, shall also be white or of bright colors, but may be of any color if not used in match play. Only club insignia, name of club, name of racquetball organization, name of tournament, or name of sponsor may be on the uniform. Players may not play without shirts.

# Part III. Officiating

**Rule 3.1—Tournaments.** All tournaments shall be managed by a committee or chairman, who shall designate the officials.

**Rule 3.2—Officials.** The officials shall include a referee and a scorer. Additional assistants and record keepers may be designated as desired.

**Rule 3.3—Qualifications.** Since the quality of the officiating often determines the success of each tournament, all officials shall be experienced or trained, and shall be thoroughly familiar with these rules and with the local playing conditions.

**Rule 3.4—Rule Briefing.** Before all tournaments, all officials and players shall be briefed on rules and on local court hinders or other regulations.

**Rule 3.5—Referees. (a) Pre-Match Duties.** Before each match commences, it shall be the duty of the referee to:

**(1)** Check on adequacy of preparation of the court with respect to cleanliness, lighting and temperature, and upon location of locker rooms, drinking fountains, etc.

**(2)** Check on availability and suitability of all materials necessary for the match, such as balls, towels, score cards, and pencils.

**(3)** Check readiness and qualifications of assisting officials.

**(4)** Explain court regulations to players and inspect the compliance of racquets with rules.

**(5)** Remind players to have an adequate supply of extra racquets and uniforms.

**(6)** Introduce players, toss coin, and signal start of first game.

**(b) Decisions.** During games the referee shall decide all questions that may arise in accordance with these rules. If there is body contact on the back swing, the player should call it quickly. This is the only call a player may make. On all questions involving judgment and on all questions not covered by these rules, the decision of the referee is final.

**(c) Protests.** Any decision not involving the judgment of the referee may on protest be decided by the chairman, if present, or his delegated representative.

**(d) Forfeitures.** A match may be forfeited by the referee when:

**(1)** Any player refuses to abide by the referee's decision, or engages in unsportsmanlike conduct.

**(2)** After warning any player leaves the court without permission of the referee during a game.

**(3)** Any player for a singles match, or any team for a doubles match, fails to report to play. Normally, 20 minutes from the scheduled game time will be allowed before forfeiture. The tournament chairman may permit a longer delay if circumstances warrant such a decision.

**(4)** If both players for a singles, or both teams for doubles, fail to appear to play for consolation matches or other play-offs, they shall forfeit their ratings for future tournaments, and forfeit any trophies, medals, awards, or prize money.

**Rule 3.5 (e) Referee's Technical.** The referee is empowered, after giving due warning, to deduct one point from a contestant's or his team's total score when in the referee's sole judgment, the contestant during the course of the match is being overtly and deliberately abusive beyond a point of reason. The warning referred to will be called a **"Technical Warning"** and the actual invoking of this penalty is called a **"Referee's Technical."** If, after the technical is called against the abusing contestant and the play is not immediately continued within the allotted time provided for under the existing rules, the referee is empowered to forfeit the match in favor of the abusing contestant's opponent or opponents, as the case may be. The **"Referee's Technical"** can be invoked by the referee as many times during the course of a match as he deems necessary.

**Rule 3.6—Scorers.** The scorer shall keep a record of the progress of the game in the manner prescribed by the committee or chairman. As a minimum the progress record shall include the order of serves, outs, and points. The referee or scorer shall announce the score before each serve.

**Rule 3.7—Record Keepers.** In addition to the scorer, the committee may designate additional persons to keep more detailed records for statistical purposes of the progress of the game.

**Rule 3.8—Linesmen.** In any U.S.R.A. or N.R.C. sanctioned tournament match, linesmen may be designated in order to help decide appealed rulings. Two linesmen will be designated by the tournament chairman, and shall at the referee's signal either agree or disagree with the referee's ruling.

The official signal by a linesman to show agreement with the referee is "thumbs up." The official signal to show disagreement is "thumbs down." The official signal for no opinion is an "open palm down."

Both linesmen must disagree with the referee in order to reverse his ruling. If one linesman agrees and one linesman disagrees or has no opinion the referee's call shall stand.

**Rule 3.9—Appeals.** In any U.S.R.A. or N.R.C. sanctioned tournament match using linesmen, a player or team may appeal certain calls by the referee. These calls are (1) kill shots (whether good or bad); (2) short serves; and (3) double-bounce pick-ups. At no time may a player or team appeal hinder, avoidable hinder, or technical foul calls.

The appeal must be directed to the referee, who will then request

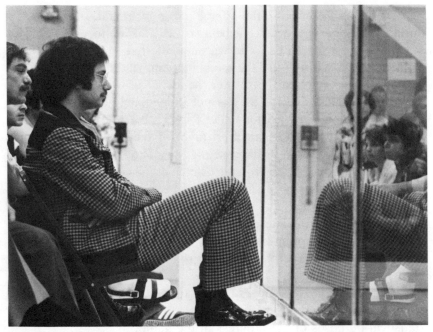

Where possible, sideline referees are used. Sometimes a vote is taken on a call, and the principal referee's vote overruled.

opinions from the linesmen. Any appeal made directly to a linesman by a player or team will be considered null and void, and forfeit any appeal rights for that player or team for that particular rally.

(a) **Kill Shot Appeals.** If the referee makes a call of "good" on a kill shot attempt which ends a particular rally, the loser of the rally may appeal the call, if he feels the shot was not good. If the appeal is successful and the referee's original call reversed, the player who originally lost the rally is declared winner of the rally and is entitled to every benefit under the rules as such, i.e., point and/or service.

If the referee makes a call of "bad" or "skip" on a kill shot attempt, he has ended the rally. The player against whom the call went has the right to appeal the call, if he feels the shot was good. If the appeal is successful and the referee's original call reversed, the player who originally lost the rally is declared winner of the rally and is enti-

140

tled to every benefit under the rules as winner of a rally.

**(b) Short Serve Appeals.** If the referee makes a call of "short" on a serve that the server felt was good, the server may appeal the call. If his appeal is successful, the server is then entitled to two additional serves.

If the served ball was considered by the referee to be an ACE serve to the crotch of the floor and side wall and in his opinion there was absolutely no way for the receiver to return the serve, then a point shall be awarded to the server.

If the referee makes a "no call" on a particular serve (therefore making it a legal serve) but either player feels the serve was short, either player may appeal the call at the end of the rally. If the loser of the rally appeals and wins his appeal, then the situation reverts back to the point of service with the call becoming "short." If it was a first service, one more serve attempt is allowed. If the server already had one fault, this second fault would cause a side out.

**(c) Double-bounce pick-up appeals.** If the referee makes a call of "two bounces," thereby stopping play, the player against whom the call was made has the right of appeal, if he feels he retrieved the ball legally. If the appeal is upheld, the rally is re-played.

If the referee makes no call on a particular play during the course of a rally in which one player feels his opponent retrieved a ball on two or more bounces, the player feeling this way has the right of appeal. However, since the ball is in play, the player wishing to appeal must clearly motion to the referee and linesmen, thereby alerting them to the exact play which is being appealed. At the same time, the player appealing must continue to retrieve and play the rally.

If the appealing player should win the rally, no appeal is necessary. If he loses the rally, and his appeal is upheld, the call is reversed and the "good" retrieve by his opponent becomes a "double-bounce pick-up," making the appealing player the winner of the rally and entitled to all benefits thereof.

**Rule 3.10—** If at any time during the course of a match the referee is of the opinion that a player or team is deliberately abusing the right of appeal, by either repetitious appeals of obvious rulings, or as a means of unsportsmanlike conduct, the referee shall enforce the Technical Foul rule.

# Part IV. Play Regulations

**Rule 4.1—Serve-Generally. (a) Order.** The player or side winning the toss becomes the first server and starts the first game, and the third game, if any.

**(b) Start.** Games are started from any place in the service zone. No part of either foot may extend beyond either line of the service zone. Stepping on the line (but not beyond it) is permitted. Server must remain in the service zone until the served ball passes short line. Violations are called "foot faults."

**(d) Manner.** A serve is commenced by bouncing the ball to the floor in the service zone, and on the first bounce the ball is struck by the server's racquet so that it hits the front wall and on the rebound hits the floor back of the short line, either with or without touching one of the side walls.

**(e) Readiness.** Serves shall not be made until the receiving side is ready, or the referee has called play ball.

**Rule 4.2—Serve-In Doubles. (a) Server.** At the beginning of each game in doubles, each side shall inform the referee of the order of service, which order shall be followed throughout the game. Only the first server serves the first time up and continues to serve first throughout the game. When the first server is out—the side is out. Thereafter both players on each side shall serve until a hand-out occurs. It is not necessary for the server to alternate serves to their opponents.

**(b) Partner's Position.** On each serve, the server's partner shall stand erect with his back to the side wall and with both feet on the floor within the service box until the served ball passes the short line. Violations are called "foot faults."

**Rule 4.3—Defective Serves.** Defective serves are of three types resulting in penalties as follows:

**(a) Dead Ball Serve.** A dead ball serve results in no penalty and the server is given another serve without cancelling a prior illegal serve.

**(b) Fault Serve.** Two fault serves results in a hand-out.

**(c) Out Serves.** An out serve results in a hand-out.

**Rule 4.4—Dead Ball Serves.** Dead ball serves do not cancel any previous illegal serve. They occur when an otherwise legal serve:

(a) **Hits Partner.** Hits the server's partner on the fly on the rebound from the front wall while the server's partner is in the service box. Any serve that touches the floor before hitting the partner in the box is a short.

(b) **Screen Balls.** Passes too close to the server or the server's partner to obstruct the view of the returning side. Any serve passing behind the server's partner and the side wall is an automatic screen.

(c) **Court Hinders.** Hits any part of the court that under local rules is a dead ball.

**Rule 4.5—Fault Serves.** The following serves are faults and any two in succession results in a hand-out:

(a) **Foot Faults.** A foot fault results:

(1) When the server leaves the service zone before the served ball passes the short line.

(2) When the server's partner leaves the service box before the served ball passes the short line.

(b) **Short Serve.** A short serve is any served ball that first hits the front wall and on the rebound hits the floor in front of the back edge of the short line either with or without touching one side wall.

(c) **Two-Side Serve.** A two-side serve is any ball served that first hits the front wall and on the rebound hits two side walls on the fly.

(d) **Ceiling Serve.** A ceiling serve is any served ball that touches the ceiling after hitting the front wall either with or without touching one side wall.

(e) **Long Serve.** A long serve is any served ball that first hits the front wall and rebounds to the back wall before touching the floor.

(f) **Out of Court Serve.** Any ball going out of the court on the serve.

**Rule 4.6—Out serves.** Any one of the following serves results in a hand-out:

(a) **Bounces.** Bouncing the ball more than three times while in the service zone before striking the ball. A bounce is a drop or throw to the floor, followed by a catch. The ball may not be bounced anywhere but on the floor within the serve zone. Accidental dropping of the ball counts as one bounce.

(b) **Missed Ball.** Any attempt to strike the ball on the first bounce that results either in a total miss or in touching any part of the server's body other than his racquet.

**(c) Non-front serve.** Any served ball that strikes the server's partner, or the ceiling, floor or side wall, before striking the front wall.

**(d) Touched Serve.** Any served ball that on the rebound from the front wall touches the server, or touches the server's partner while any part of his body is out of the service box, or the server's partner intentionally catches the served ball on the fly.

**(e) Out-of-Order Serve.** In doubles, when either partner serves out of order.

**(f) Crotch Serve.** If the served ball hits the crotch in the front wall it is considered the same as hitting the floor and is an out. A crotch serve into the back wall is good and in play.

**Rule 4.7—Return of Serve. (a) Receiving Position.** The receiver or receivers must stand at least 5 feet back of the short line, as indicated by the 3-inch vertical line on each side wall, and cannot return the ball until it passes the short line. Any infraction results in a point for the server.

**(b) Defective Serve.** To eliminate any misunderstanding, the receiving side should not catch or touch a defectively served ball until called by the referee or it has touched the floor the second time.

**(c) Fly Return.** In making a fly return the receiver must end up with both feet back of the service zone. A violation by a receiver results in a point for the server.

**(d) Legal Return.** After the ball is legally served, one of the players on the receiving side must strike the ball with his racquet either on the fly or after the first bounce and before the ball touches the floor the second time to return the ball to the front wall either directly or after touching one or both side walls, the back wall or the ceiling, or any combination of those surfaces. A returned ball may not touch the floor before touching the front wall. (1) It is legal to return the ball by striking the ball into the back wall first, then hitting the front wall on the fly or after hitting the side wall or ceiling.

**(e) Failure to Return.** The failure to return a serve results in a point for the server.

**Rule 4.8—Changes of Serve. (a) Hand-out.** A server is entitled to continue serving until:

**(1) Out Serve.** He makes an out serve under Rule 4.6 or

144

**(2) Fault Serves.** He makes two fault serves in succession under Rule 4.5, or

**(3) Hits Partner.** He hits his partner with an attempted return before the ball touches the floor the second time, or

**(4) Return Failure.** He or his partner fails to keep the ball in play by returning it as required by Rule 4.7(d), or

**(5) Avoidable Hinder.** He or his partner commits an avoidable hinder under Rule 4.11.

**(b) Side-out (1) In Singles.** In singles, retiring the server retires the side.

**(2) In Doubles.** In doubles, the side is retired when both partners have been put out, except on the first serve as provided in Rule 4.2(a).

**(c) Effect.** When the server on the side loses the serve, the server or serving side shall become the receiver; and the receiving side, the server; and so alternately in all subsequent services of the game.

**Rule 4.9—Volleys.** Each legal return after the serve is called a volley. Play during volleys shall be according to the following rules:

**(a) One or both Hands.** Only the head of the racquet may be used at any time to return the ball. The ball must be hit with the racquet in one or both hands. Switching hands to hit a ball is out. The use of any portion of the body is an out.

**(b) One Touch.** In attempting returns, the ball may be touched only once by one player on returning side. In doubles both partners may swing at, but only one may hit, the ball. Each violation of (a) or (b) results in a hand-out or point.

**(c) Return Attempts. (1) In Singles.** In singles if a player swings at but misses the ball in play, the player may repeat his attempts to return the ball until it touches the floor the second time.

**(2) In Doubles.** In doubles if one player swings at but misses the ball, both he and his partner may make further attempts to return the ball until it touches the floor the second time. Both partners on a side are entitled to an attempt to return the ball.

**(3) Hinders.** In singles or doubles, if a player swings at but misses the ball in play, and in his or his partner's attempt again to play the ball there is an unintentional interference by an opponent it shall be a hinder. (See Rule 4.10.)

145

If you miss the ball completely, you can swing again until you hit it.

**(d) Touching Ball.** Except as provided in Rule 4.10(a) (2), any touching of a ball before it touches the floor the second time by a player other than the one making a return is a point or out against the offending player.

146

**(e) Out of Court Ball. (1) After Return.** Any ball returned to the front wall which on the rebound or on the first bounce goes into the gallery or through any opening in a side wall shall be declared dead and the serve replayed.

**(2) No Return.** Any ball not returned to the front wall, but which caroms off a player's racquet into the gallery or into any opening in a side wall either with or without touching the ceiling, side or back wall, shall be an out or point against the players failing to make the return.

**(f) Dry Ball.** During the game and particularly on service every effort should be made to keep the ball dry. Deliberately wetting shall result in an out. The ball may be inspected by the referee at any time during a game.

**(g) Broken Ball.** If there is any suspicion that a ball has broken on the serve or during a volley, play shall continue until the end of the volley. The referee or any player may request the ball be examined. If the referee decides the ball is broken or otherwise defective, a new ball shall be put into play and the point replayed.

**(h) Play Stoppage.** (1) If a player loses a shoe or other equipment, or foreign objects enter the court, or any other outside interference occurs, the referee shall stop the play. (2) If a player loses control of his racquet, time should be called after the point has been decided, providing the racquet does not strike an opponent or interfere with ensuing play.

**Rule 4.10—Dead Ball Hinders.** Hinders are of two types—"dead ball" and "avoidable." Dead ball hinders, described in this rule, result in the point being replayed. Avoidable hinders are described in Rule 4.11.

**(a) Situations.** When called by the referee, the following are dead ball hinders:

**(1) Court Hinders.** Hits any part of the court which under local rules is a dead ball.

**(2) Hitting Opponent.** Any returned ball that touches an opponent on the fly before it returns to the front wall.

**(3) Body Contact.** Any body contact with an opponent that interferes with seeing or returning the ball.

**(4) Screen Ball.** Any ball rebounding from the front wall close to the body of a player on the side which just returned the ball, to interfere with

147

or prevent the returning side from seeing the ball. See Rule 4.4(b).

**(5) Straddle Ball.** A ball passing between the legs of a player on the side which just returned the ball, if there is no fair chance to see or return the ball.

**(6) Other Interference.** Any other unintentional interference which prevents an opponent from having a fair chance to see or return the ball.

**(b) Effect.** A call by the referee of a "hinder" stops the play and voids any situation following, such as the ball hitting a player. No player is authorized to call a hinder, except on the back swing and such a call must be made immediately as provided in Rule 3.5(b).

**(c) Avoidance.** While making an attempt to return the ball, a player is entitled to a fair chance to see and return the ball. It is the duty of the side that has just served or returned the ball to move so that the receiving side may go straight to the ball and not be required to go around an opponent. The referee should be liberal in calling hinders to discourage any practice of playing the ball where an adversary cannot see it until too late. It is no excuse that the ball is "killed," unless in the opinion of the referee he couldn't return the ball. Hinders should be called without a claim by a player, especially in close plays and on game points.

**(d) In Doubles.** In doubles, both players on a side are entitled to a fair and unobstructed chance at the ball and either one is entitled to a hinder even though it naturally would be his partner's ball and even though his partner may have attempted to play the ball or that he may already have missed it. It is not a hinder when one player hinders his partner.

**Rule 4.11—Avoidable Hinders.** An avoidable hinder results in an "out" or a point depending upon whether the offender was serving or receiving.

**(a) Failure to Move.** Does not move sufficiently to allow opponent his shot.

**(b) Blocking.** Moves into a position effecting a block, on the opponent about to return the ball, or, in doubles, one partner moves in front of an opponent as his partner is returning the ball.

**(c) Moving into Ball.** Moves in the way and is struck by the ball just played by his opponent.

**(d) Pushing.** Deliberately pushing or shoving an opponent during a volley.

148

Even the Master—Brumfield—sometimes causes a hinder.

**Rule 4.12—Rest Periods. (a) Delays.** Deliberate delay exceeding ten seconds by server or receiver shall result in an out or point against the offender.

**(b) During Game.** During a game each player in singles, or each side in doubles, either while serving or receiving, may request a "time out" for a towel, wiping glasses, change or adjustment. Each "time out" shall not exceed 30 seconds. No more than three "time outs" in a game shall be granted each singles player or each team in doubles.

**(c) Injury.** No time out shall be charged to a player who is injured during play. An injured player shall not be allowed more than a total of 15 minutes of rest. If the injured player is not able to resume play after total rests of 15 minutes the match shall be awarded to the opponent or opponents. On any further injury to same player, the Commissioner, if present, or committee, after considering any available medical opinion shall determine whether the injured player will be allowed to continue.

**(d) Between Games.** A five-minute rest period is allowed between the first and second games and a 10-minute rest period between the second and third games. Players may leave the court between games, but must be on the court and ready to play at the expiration of the rest period.

**(e) Postponed Games.** Any games postponed by referee due to weather elements shall be resumed with the same score as when postponed.

## Part V. Tournaments

**Rule 5.1—Draws.** The seeding method of drawing shall be the standard method approved by the U.S.R.A. and N.R.C. All draws in professional brackets shall be the responsibility of the National Director of the N.R.C.

**Rule 5.2—Scheduling (a) Preliminary Matches.** If one or more contestants are entered in both singles and doubles they may be required to play both singles and doubles on the same day or night with little rest between matches. This is a risk assumed on entering both singles and doubles. If possible the schedule should provide at least a one-hour rest period between all matches.

**(b) Final Matches.** Where one or more players have reached the finals in both singles and doubles, it is recommended that the doubles match be played on the day preceding the singles. This would assume more rest between the final matches. If both final matches must be played on the same day or night, the following procedure shall be followed:

**(1)** The singles match be played first.

**(2)** A rest period of not less than ONE HOUR be allowed between the finals in singles and doubles.

**Rule 5.3—Notice of Matches.** After the first round of matches, it is the responsibility of each player to check the posted schedules to determine the time and place of each subsequent match. If any change is made in the schedule after posting, it shall be the duty of the committee or chairman to notify the players of the change.

**Rule 5.4—Third Place.** In championship tournaments: national, state, district, etc. (if there is a playoff for third place), the loser in the semi-finals must play for third place or lose his ranking for the next year unless he is unable to compete because of injury or illness. See Rule 3.5(d) (4).

**Rule 5.5—U.S.R.A. Regional Tournaments.** Each year the United States and Canada are divided into regions for the purpose of sectional competition preceding the National Championships. The exact boundaries of each region are dependent on the location of the regional tournaments. Such locations are announced in NATIONAL RACQUET-BALL magazine.

**(a)** Only players residing in the area defined can participate in a regional tournament.

**(b)** Players can participate in only one event in a regional tournament.

**(c)** Winners of open singles in regional tournaments will receive round trip air coach tickets to the U.S.R.A. national tourney. Remuneration will be made after arrival at the Nationals.

**(d)** A U.S.R.A. officer will be in attendance at each regional tournament and will coordinate with the host chairman.

**Awards:** No individual award in U.S.R.A.-sanctioned tournaments should exceed value of more than $25.

**Tournament Management:** In all U.S.R.A.-sanctioned tournaments the tournament chairman and/or the national U.S.R.A. official in attendance may decide on a change of courts after the completion of any tournament game if such a change will accommodate better spectator conditions.

**Tournament Conduct:** In all U.S.R.A.-sanctioned tournaments the referee is empowered to default a match if an individual player or team conducts itself to the detriment of the tournament and the game.

**Professional Definition:** Any player who has accepted $200 or more in prizes and/or prize money in the most recent 12 calendar months is considered a professional racquetball player and ineligible for participation in any U.S.R.A.-sanctioned tournament bracket.

**Amateur Definition:** We hold as eligible for amateur racquetball tournaments sanctioned by the U.S.R.A. anyone except those who qualify as professionals under current U.S.R.A.-N.R.C. rules.

**Pick-A-Partner:** The essence of the "Players' Fraternity" has been to allow players to come to tournaments and select a partner, if necessary, regardless of what organization or city he might represent.

**Age Brackets:** The following age brackets, determined by the age of the player on the first day of the tournament, are:

**Open:** Any age can compete.

**Juniors:** 18 and under.

**Seniors:** 35 and over.

**Masters:** 45 and over.

**Golden Masters:** 55 and over.

In doubles both players must be within the specified age bracket.


# ONE-WALL AND THREE-WALL RULES

Basically racquetball rules for one-wall, three-wall and four-wall are the same with the following exceptions:

*One-Wall*—**Court Size**—Wall shall be 20 ft. in width and 16 ft. high, floor 20 ft. in width and 34 ft. from the wall to back edge of the long line. There should be a minimum of 3 feet beyond the long line and 6 feet outside each side line. There should be a minimum of 6 feet outside each side line and behind the long line to permit movement area for the players.

**Short Line**—Back edge 16 feet from the wall. Service Markers— Lines at least 6 inches long parallel to and midway between the long and short lines, extending in from the side lines. The imaginary extension and joining of these lines indicates the service line. Lines are 1½ inches in width. Service Zone—floor area inside and including the short side and service lines. Receiving Zone—floor area in back of short line bounded by and including the long and side lines.

*Three-Wall*—**Serve**—A serve that goes beyond the side walls on the fly is player or side out. A serve that goes beyond the long line on a fly but within the side walls is the same as a ''short.''

# photo essay:
# marty hogan at
# the new england pro-am

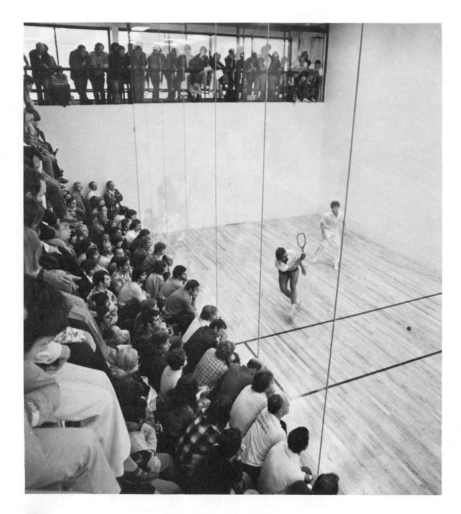

The souvenir program for the New England Pro-Am Tournament in Burlington, Vermont, had it right. A small picture of Marty Hogan was captioned: "The youngest pro racquetballer in the nation, this 17-year-old is the player to watch if the fans are hoping for an upset."

An upset of whom? Only the handful of best players in the country—Charlie Brumfield, the current National Champ; Steve Serot, the 19-year-old all-time leading money winner on the tour; and super-pro Steve Keeley. To say nothing of the likes of Steve Strandemo, Bill Schmidtke, and Rich Wagner, all present. A win over any of these aces would have satisfied any other player in the country. But not Hogan. "I'm going to beat them all," he predicted.

After a shaky start, Hogan ran all over Brumfield, two games to one. At 20-5, match point, borrowing some of Brumfield's traditionally cool psyching, he yelled, "Will somebody get my mother on the phone?"

156

marty hogan

"If I don't dive," Steve Serot said, "I'm not worth anything. It's my game." One of those dives injured his playing elbow. After a 15-minute injury break he came back, but he couldn't top Hogan.

In the finals against Keeley, Hogan came from behind, fired up, and won 21-13, 21-17. "I was just tired of losing to all these guys in past tournaments," said Hogan.

After his victory, National Commissioner and Business Manager Joe Ardito congratulated him as an autograph fan waited, and champion Schmidtke came up to shake.

In the locker room, Brumfield good-naturedly showed Hogan what his problem was: Hogan's serve, for one. Hogan is a worrier. "Can I do it again?" (Several months later he replayed his victory in Milwaukee.)

There is nothing tougher than practice or sweeter than being number one. Even number one in your local club, or among your racquetball friends. If a mere 17-year-old could do it—so can you! Good luck.

# index

# index